CMA

Financial Reporting, Planning, Performance, and Control Exam

Secrets Study Guide

Part 1

DEAR FUTURE EXAM SUCCESS STORY

First of all, **THANK YOU** for purchasing Mometrix study materials!

Second, congratulations! You are one of the few determined test-takers who are committed to doing whatever it takes to excel on your exam. **You have come to the right place.** We developed these study materials with one goal in mind: to deliver you the information you need in a format that's concise and easy to use.

In addition to optimizing your guide for the content of the test, we've outlined our recommended steps for breaking down the preparation process into small, attainable goals so you can make sure you stay on track.

We've also analyzed the entire test-taking process, identifying the most common pitfalls and showing how you can overcome them and be ready for any curveball the test throws you.

Standardized testing is one of the biggest obstacles on your road to success, which only increases the importance of doing well in the high-pressure, high-stakes environment of test day. Your results on this test could have a significant impact on your future, and this guide provides the information and practical advice to help you achieve your full potential on test day.

Your success is our success

We would love to hear from you! If you would like to share the story of your exam success or if you have any questions or comments in regard to our products, please contact us at **800-673-8175** or **support@mometrix.com**.

Thanks again for your business and we wish you continued success!

Sincerely,
The Mometrix Test Preparation Team

Need more help? Check out our flashcards at:
http://MometrixFlashcards.com/CMA

Written and edited by the Mometrix Exam Secrets Test Prep Team
Printed in the United States of America

Table of Contents

Introduction

Thank you for purchasing this resource! You have made the choice to prepare yourself for a test that could have a huge impact on your future, and this guide is designed to help you be fully ready for test day. Obviously, it's important to have a solid understanding of the test material, but you also need to be prepared for the unique environment and stressors of the test, so that you can perform to the best of your abilities.

For this purpose, the first section that appears in this guide is the **Secret Keys**. We've devoted countless hours to meticulously researching what works and what doesn't, and we've boiled down our findings to the five most impactful steps you can take to improve your performance on the test. We start at the beginning with study planning and move through the preparation process, all the way to the testing strategies that will help you get the most out of what you know when you're finally sitting in front of the test.

We recommend that you start preparing for your test as far in advance as possible. However, if you've bought this guide as a last-minute study resource and only have a few days before your test, we recommend that you skip over the first two Secret Keys since they address a long-term study plan.

If you struggle with **test anxiety**, we strongly encourage you to check out our recommendations for how you can overcome it. Test anxiety is a formidable foe, but it can be beaten, and we want to make sure you have the tools you need to defeat it.

Secret Key #1 – Plan Big, Study Small

There's a lot riding on your performance. If you want to ace this test, you're going to need to keep your skills sharp and the material fresh in your mind. You need a plan that lets you review everything you need to know while still fitting in your schedule. We'll break this strategy down into three categories.

Information Organization

Start with the information you already have: the official test outline. From this, you can make a complete list of all the concepts you need to cover before the test. Organize these concepts into groups that can be studied together, and create a list of any related vocabulary you need to learn so you can brush up on any difficult terms. You'll want to keep this vocabulary list handy once you actually start studying since you may need to add to it along the way.

Time Management

Once you have your set of study concepts, decide how to spread them out over the time you have left before the test. Break your study plan into small, clear goals so you have a manageable task for each day and know exactly what you're doing. Then just focus on one small step at a time. When you manage your time this way, you don't need to spend hours at a time studying. Studying a small block of content for a short period each day helps you retain information better and avoid stressing over how much you have left to do. You can relax knowing that you have a plan to cover everything in time. In order for this strategy to be effective though, you have to start studying early and stick to your schedule. Avoid the exhaustion and futility that comes from last-minute cramming!

Study Environment

The environment you study in has a big impact on your learning. Studying in a coffee shop, while probably more enjoyable, is not likely to be as fruitful as studying in a quiet room. It's important to keep distractions to a minimum. You're only planning to study for a short block of time, so make the most of it. Don't pause to check your phone or get up to find a snack. It's also important to **avoid multitasking**. Research has consistently shown that multitasking will make your studying dramatically less effective. Your study area should also be comfortable and well-lit so you don't have the distraction of straining your eyes or sitting on an uncomfortable chair.

The time of day you study is also important. You want to be rested and alert. Don't wait until just before bedtime. Study when you'll be most likely to comprehend and remember. Even better, if you know what time of day your test will be, set that time aside for study. That way your brain will be used to working on that subject at that specific time and you'll have a better chance of recalling information.

Finally, it can be helpful to team up with others who are studying for the same test. Your actual studying should be done in as isolated an environment as possible, but the work of organizing the information and setting up the study plan can be divided up. In between study sessions, you can discuss with your teammates the concepts that you're all studying and quiz each other on the details. Just be sure that your teammates are as serious about the test as you are. If you find that your study time is being replaced with social time, you might need to find a new team.

Secret Key #2 – Make Your Studying Count

You're devoting a lot of time and effort to preparing for this test, so you want to be absolutely certain it will pay off. This means doing more than just reading the content and hoping you can remember it on test day. It's important to make every minute of study count. There are two main areas you can focus on to make your studying count.

Retention

It doesn't matter how much time you study if you can't remember the material. You need to make sure you are retaining the concepts. To check your retention of the information you're learning, try recalling it at later times with minimal prompting. Try carrying around flashcards and glance at one or two from time to time or ask a friend who's also studying for the test to quiz you.

To enhance your retention, look for ways to put the information into practice so that you can apply it rather than simply recalling it. If you're using the information in practical ways, it will be much easier to remember. Similarly, it helps to solidify a concept in your mind if you're not only reading it to yourself but also explaining it to someone else. Ask a friend to let you teach them about a concept you're a little shaky on (or speak aloud to an imaginary audience if necessary). As you try to summarize, define, give examples, and answer your friend's questions, you'll understand the concepts better and they will stay with you longer. Finally, step back for a big picture view and ask yourself how each piece of information fits with the whole subject. When you link the different concepts together and see them working together as a whole, it's easier to remember the individual components.

Finally, practice showing your work on any multi-step problems, even if you're just studying. Writing out each step you take to solve a problem will help solidify the process in your mind, and you'll be more likely to remember it during the test.

Modality

Modality simply refers to the means or method by which you study. Choosing a study modality that fits your own individual learning style is crucial. No two people learn best in exactly the same way, so it's important to know your strengths and use them to your advantage.

For example, if you learn best by visualization, focus on visualizing a concept in your mind and draw an image or a diagram. Try color-coding your notes, illustrating them, or creating symbols that will trigger your mind to recall a learned concept. If you learn best by hearing or discussing information, find a study partner who learns the same way or read aloud to yourself. Think about how to put the information in your own words. Imagine that you are giving a lecture on the topic and record yourself so you can listen to it later.

For any learning style, flashcards can be helpful. Organize the information so you can take advantage of spare moments to review. Underline key words or phrases. Use different colors for different categories. Mnemonic devices (such as creating a short list in which every item starts with the same letter) can also help with retention. Find what works best for you and use it to store the information in your mind most effectively and easily.

Secret Key #3 – Practice the Right Way

Your success on test day depends not only on how many hours you put into preparing, but also on whether you prepared the right way. It's good to check along the way to see if your studying is paying off. One of the most effective ways to do this is by taking practice tests to evaluate your progress. Practice tests are useful because they show exactly where you need to improve. Every time you take a practice test, pay special attention to these three groups of questions:

- The questions you got wrong
- The questions you had to guess on, even if you guessed right
- The questions you found difficult or slow to work through

This will show you exactly what your weak areas are, and where you need to devote more study time. Ask yourself why each of these questions gave you trouble. Was it because you didn't understand the material? Was it because you didn't remember the vocabulary? Do you need more repetitions on this type of question to build speed and confidence? Dig into those questions and figure out how you can strengthen your weak areas as you go back to review the material.

Additionally, many practice tests have a section explaining the answer choices. It can be tempting to read the explanation and think that you now have a good understanding of the concept. However, an explanation likely only covers part of the question's broader context. Even if the explanation makes perfect sense, **go back and investigate** every concept related to the question until you're positive you have a thorough understanding.

As you go along, keep in mind that the practice test is just that: practice. Memorizing these questions and answers will not be very helpful on the actual test because it is unlikely to have any of the same exact questions. If you only know the right answers to the sample questions, you won't be prepared for the real thing. **Study the concepts** until you understand them fully, and then you'll be able to answer any question that shows up on the test.

It's important to wait on the practice tests until you're ready. If you take a test on your first day of study, you may be overwhelmed by the amount of material covered and how much you need to learn. Work up to it gradually.

On test day, you'll need to be prepared for answering questions, managing your time, and using the test-taking strategies you've learned. It's a lot to balance, like a mental marathon that will have a big impact on your future. Like training for a marathon, you'll need to start slowly and work your way up. When test day arrives, you'll be ready.

Start with the strategies you've read in the first two Secret Keys—plan your course and study in the way that works best for you. If you have time, consider using multiple study resources to get different approaches to the same concepts. It can be helpful to see difficult concepts from more than one angle. Then find a good source for practice tests. Many times, the test website will suggest potential study resources or provide sample tests.

Practice Test Strategy

If you're able to find at least three practice tests, we recommend this strategy:

Untimed and Open-Book Practice

Take the first test with no time constraints and with your notes and study guide handy. Take your time and focus on applying the strategies you've learned.

Timed and Open-Book Practice

Take the second practice test open-book as well, but set a timer and practice pacing yourself to finish in time.

Timed and Closed-Book Practice

Take any other practice tests as if it were test day. Set a timer and put away your study materials. Sit at a table or desk in a quiet room, imagine yourself at the testing center, and answer questions as quickly and accurately as possible.

Keep repeating timed and closed-book tests on a regular basis until you run out of practice tests or it's time for the actual test. Your mind will be ready for the schedule and stress of test day, and you'll be able to focus on recalling the material you've learned.

Secret Key #4 – Pace Yourself

Once you're fully prepared for the material on the test, your biggest challenge on test day will be managing your time. Just knowing that the clock is ticking can make you panic even if you have plenty of time left. Work on pacing yourself so you can build confidence against the time constraints of the exam. Pacing is a difficult skill to master, especially in a high-pressure environment, so **practice is vital**.

Set time expectations for your pace based on how much time is available. For example, if a section has 60 questions and the time limit is 30 minutes, you know you have to average 30 seconds or less per question in order to answer them all. Although 30 seconds is the hard limit, set 25 seconds per question as your goal, so you reserve extra time to spend on harder questions. When you budget extra time for the harder questions, you no longer have any reason to stress when those questions take longer to answer.

Don't let this time expectation distract you from working through the test at a calm, steady pace, but keep it in mind so you don't spend too much time on any one question. Recognize that taking extra time on one question you don't understand may keep you from answering two that you do understand later in the test. If your time limit for a question is up and you're still not sure of the answer, mark it and move on, and come back to it later if the time and the test format allow. If the testing format doesn't allow you to return to earlier questions, just make an educated guess; then put it out of your mind and move on.

On the easier questions, be careful not to rush. It may seem wise to hurry through them so you have more time for the challenging ones, but it's not worth missing one if you know the concept and just didn't take the time to read the question fully. Work efficiently but make sure you understand the question and have looked at all of the answer choices, since more than one may seem right at first.

Even if you're paying attention to the time, you may find yourself a little behind at some point. You should speed up to get back on track, but do so wisely. Don't panic; just take a few seconds less on each question until you're caught up. Don't guess without thinking, but do look through the answer choices and eliminate any you know are wrong. If you can get down to two choices, it is often worthwhile to guess from those. Once you've chosen an answer, move on and don't dwell on any that you skipped or had to hurry through. If a question was taking too long, chances are it was one of the harder ones, so you weren't as likely to get it right anyway.

On the other hand, if you find yourself getting ahead of schedule, it may be beneficial to slow down a little. The more quickly you work, the more likely you are to make a careless mistake that will affect your score. You've budgeted time for each question, so don't be afraid to spend that time. Practice an efficient but careful pace to get the most out of the time you have.

Secret Key #5 – Have a Plan for Guessing

When you're taking the test, you may find yourself stuck on a question. Some of the answer choices seem better than others, but you don't see the one answer choice that is obviously correct. What do you do?

The scenario described above is very common, yet most test takers have not effectively prepared for it. Developing and practicing a plan for guessing may be one of the single most effective uses of your time as you get ready for the exam.

In developing your plan for guessing, there are three questions to address:

- When should you start the guessing process?
- How should you narrow down the choices?
- Which answer should you choose?

When to Start the Guessing Process

Unless your plan for guessing is to select C every time (which, despite its merits, is not what we recommend), you need to leave yourself enough time to apply your answer elimination strategies. Since you have a limited amount of time for each question, that means that if you're going to give yourself the best shot at guessing correctly, you have to decide quickly whether or not you will guess.

Of course, the best-case scenario is that you don't have to guess at all, so first, see if you can answer the question based on your knowledge of the subject and basic reasoning skills. Focus on the key words in the question and try to jog your memory of related topics. Give yourself a chance to bring the knowledge to mind, but once you realize that you don't have (or you can't access) the knowledge you need to answer the question, it's time to start the guessing process.

It's almost always better to start the guessing process too early than too late. It only takes a few seconds to remember something and answer the question from knowledge. Carefully eliminating wrong answer choices takes longer. Plus, going through the process of eliminating answer choices can actually help jog your memory.

Summary: Start the guessing process as soon as you decide that you can't answer the question based on your knowledge.

How to Narrow Down the Choices

The next chapter in this book (**Test-Taking Strategies**) includes a wide range of strategies for how to approach questions and how to look for answer choices to eliminate. You will definitely want to read those carefully, practice them, and figure out which ones work best for you. Here though, we're going to address a mindset rather than a particular strategy.

Your odds of guessing an answer correctly depend on how many options you are choosing from.

Number of options left	5	4	3	2	1
Odds of guessing correctly	20%	25%	33%	50%	100%

You can see from this chart just how valuable it is to be able to eliminate incorrect answers and make an educated guess, but there are two things that many test takers do that cause them to miss out on the benefits of guessing:

- Accidentally eliminating the correct answer
- Selecting an answer based on an impression

We'll look at the first one here, and the second one in the next section.

To avoid accidentally eliminating the correct answer, we recommend a thought exercise called **the $5 challenge**. In this challenge, you only eliminate an answer choice from contention if you are willing to bet $5 on it being wrong. Why $5? Five dollars is a small but not insignificant amount of money. It's an amount you could afford to lose but wouldn't want to throw away. And while losing $5 once might not hurt too much, doing it twenty times will set you back $100. In the same way, each small decision you make—eliminating a choice here, guessing on a question there—won't by itself impact your score very much, but when you put them all together, they can make a big difference. By holding each answer choice elimination decision to a higher standard, you can reduce the risk of accidentally eliminating the correct answer.

The $5 challenge can also be applied in a positive sense: If you are willing to bet $5 that an answer choice *is* correct, go ahead and mark it as correct.

Summary: Only eliminate an answer choice if you are willing to bet $5 that it is wrong.

Which Answer to Choose

You're taking the test. You've run into a hard question and decided you'll have to guess. You've eliminated all the answer choices you're willing to bet $5 on. Now you have to pick an answer. Why do we even need to talk about this? Why can't you just pick whichever one you feel like when the time comes?

The answer to these questions is that if you don't come into the test with a plan, you'll rely on your impression to select an answer choice, and if you do that, you risk falling into a trap. The test writers know that everyone who takes their test will be guessing on some of the questions, so they intentionally write wrong answer choices to seem plausible. You still have to pick an answer though, and if the wrong answer choices are designed to look right, how can you ever be sure that you're not falling for their trap? The best solution we've found to this dilemma is to take the decision out of your hands entirely. Here is the process we recommend:

Once you've eliminated any choices that you are confident (willing to bet $5) are wrong, select the first remaining choice as your answer.

Whether you choose to select the first remaining choice, the second, or the last, the important thing is that you use some preselected standard. Using this approach guarantees that you will not be enticed into selecting an answer choice that looks right, because you are not basing your decision on how the answer choices look.

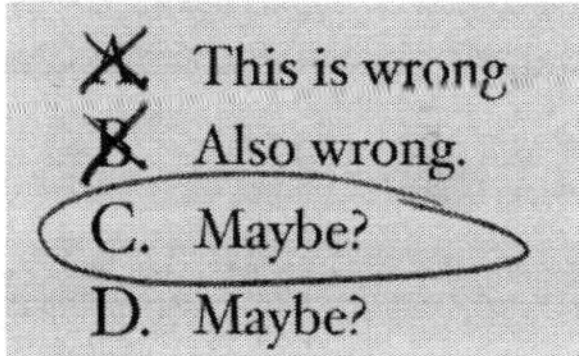

This is not meant to make you question your knowledge. Instead, it is to help you recognize the difference between your knowledge and your impressions. There's a huge difference between thinking an answer is right because of what you know, and thinking an answer is right because it looks or sounds like it should be right.

Summary: To ensure that your selection is appropriately random, make a predetermined selection from among all answer choices you have not eliminated.

Test-Taking Strategies

This section contains a list of test-taking strategies that you may find helpful as you work through the test. By taking what you know and applying logical thought, you can maximize your chances of answering any question correctly!

It is very important to realize that every question is different and every person is different: no single strategy will work on every question, and no single strategy will work for every person. That's why we've included all of them here, so you can try them out and determine which ones work best for different types of questions and which ones work best for you.

Question Strategies

✓ Read Carefully

Read the question and the answer choices carefully. Don't miss the question because you misread the terms. You have plenty of time to read each question thoroughly and make sure you understand what is being asked. Yet a happy medium must be attained, so don't waste too much time. You must read carefully and efficiently.

✓ Contextual Clues

Look for contextual clues. If the question includes a word you are not familiar with, look at the immediate context for some indication of what the word might mean. Contextual clues can often give you all the information you need to decipher the meaning of an unfamiliar word. Even if you can't determine the meaning, you may be able to narrow down the possibilities enough to make a solid guess at the answer to the question.

✓ Prefixes

If you're having trouble with a word in the question or answer choices, try dissecting it. Take advantage of every clue that the word might include. Prefixes can be a huge help. Usually, they allow you to determine a basic meaning. *Pre-* means before, *post-* means after, *pro-* is positive, *de-* is negative. From prefixes, you can get an idea of the general meaning of the word and try to put it into context.

✓ Hedge Words

Watch out for critical hedge words, such as *likely, may, can, sometimes, often, almost, mostly, usually, generally, rarely*, and *sometimes*. Question writers insert these hedge phrases to cover every possibility. Often an answer choice will be wrong simply because it leaves no room for exception. Be on guard for answer choices that have definitive words such as *exactly* and *always*.

✓ Switchback Words

Stay alert for *switchbacks*. These are the words and phrases frequently used to alert you to shifts in thought. The most common switchback words are *but, although*, and *however*. Others include *nevertheless, on the other hand, even though, while, in spite of, despite*, and *regardless of*. Switchback words are important to catch because they can change the direction of the question or an answer choice.

☑ FACE VALUE

When in doubt, use common sense. Accept the situation in the problem at face value. Don't read too much into it. These problems will not require you to make wild assumptions. If you have to go beyond creativity and warp time or space in order to have an answer choice fit the question, then you should move on and consider the other answer choices. These are normal problems rooted in reality. The applicable relationship or explanation may not be readily apparent, but it is there for you to figure out. Use your common sense to interpret anything that isn't clear.

Answer Choice Strategies

☑ ANSWER SELECTION

The most thorough way to pick an answer choice is to identify and eliminate wrong answers until only one is left, then confirm it is the correct answer. Sometimes an answer choice may immediately seem right, but be careful. The test writers will usually put more than one reasonable answer choice on each question, so take a second to read all of them and make sure that the other choices are not equally obvious. As long as you have time left, it is better to read every answer choice than to pick the first one that looks right without checking the others.

☑ ANSWER CHOICE FAMILIES

An answer choice family consists of two (in rare cases, three) answer choices that are very similar in construction and cannot all be true at the same time. If you see two answer choices that are direct opposites or parallels, one of them is usually the correct answer. For instance, if one answer choice says that quantity *x* increases and another either says that quantity *x* decreases (opposite) or says that quantity *y* increases (parallel), then those answer choices would fall into the same family. An answer choice that doesn't match the construction of the answer choice family is more likely to be incorrect. Most questions will not have answer choice families, but when they do appear, you should be prepared to recognize them.

☑ ELIMINATE ANSWERS

Eliminate answer choices as soon as you realize they are wrong, but make sure you consider all possibilities. If you are eliminating answer choices and realize that the last one you are left with is also wrong, don't panic. Start over and consider each choice again. There may be something you missed the first time that you will realize on the second pass.

☑ AVOID FACT TRAPS

Don't be distracted by an answer choice that is factually true but doesn't answer the question. You are looking for the choice that answers the question. Stay focused on what the question is asking for so you don't accidentally pick an answer that is true but incorrect. Always go back to the question and make sure the answer choice you've selected actually answers the question and is not merely a true statement.

☑ EXTREME STATEMENTS

In general, you should avoid answers that put forth extreme actions as standard practice or proclaim controversial ideas as established fact. An answer choice that states the "process should be used in certain situations, if..." is much more likely to be correct than one that states the "process should be discontinued completely." The first is a calm rational statement and doesn't even make a definitive, uncompromising stance, using a hedge word *if* to provide wiggle room, whereas the second choice is far more extreme.

⊘ Benchmark

As you read through the answer choices and you come across one that seems to answer the question well, mentally select that answer choice. This is not your final answer, but it's the one that will help you evaluate the other answer choices. The one that you selected is your benchmark or standard for judging each of the other answer choices. Every other answer choice must be compared to your benchmark. That choice is correct until proven otherwise by another answer choice beating it. If you find a better answer, then that one becomes your new benchmark. Once you've decided that no other choice answers the question as well as your benchmark, you have your final answer.

⊘ Predict the Answer

Before you even start looking at the answer choices, it is often best to try to predict the answer. When you come up with the answer on your own, it is easier to avoid distractions and traps because you will know exactly what to look for. The right answer choice is unlikely to be word-for-word what you came up with, but it should be a close match. Even if you are confident that you have the right answer, you should still take the time to read each option before moving on.

General Strategies

⊘ Tough Questions

If you are stumped on a problem or it appears too hard or too difficult, don't waste time. Move on! Remember though, if you can quickly check for obviously incorrect answer choices, your chances of guessing correctly are greatly improved. Before you completely give up, at least try to knock out a couple of possible answers. Eliminate what you can and then guess at the remaining answer choices before moving on.

⊘ Check Your Work

Since you will probably not know every term listed and the answer to every question, it is important that you get credit for the ones that you do know. Don't miss any questions through careless mistakes. If at all possible, try to take a second to look back over your answer selection and make sure you've selected the correct answer choice and haven't made a costly careless mistake (such as marking an answer choice that you didn't mean to mark). This quick double check should more than pay for itself in caught mistakes for the time it costs.

⊘ Pace Yourself

It's easy to be overwhelmed when you're looking at a page full of questions; your mind is confused and full of random thoughts, and the clock is ticking down faster than you would like. Calm down and maintain the pace that you have set for yourself. Especially as you get down to the last few minutes of the test, don't let the small numbers on the clock make you panic. As long as you are on track by monitoring your pace, you are guaranteed to have time for each question.

⊘ Don't Rush

It is very easy to make errors when you are in a hurry. Maintaining a fast pace in answering questions is pointless if it makes you miss questions that you would have gotten right otherwise. Test writers like to include distracting information and wrong answers that seem right. Taking a little extra time to avoid careless mistakes can make all the difference in your test score. Find a pace that allows you to be confident in the answers that you select.

⊘ Keep Moving

Panicking will not help you pass the test, so do your best to stay calm and keep moving. Taking deep breaths and going through the answer elimination steps you practiced can help to break through a stress barrier and keep your pace.

Final Notes

The combination of a solid foundation of content knowledge and the confidence that comes from practicing your plan for applying that knowledge is the key to maximizing your performance on test day. As your foundation of content knowledge is built up and strengthened, you'll find that the strategies included in this chapter become more and more effective in helping you quickly sift through the distractions and traps of the test to isolate the correct answer.

Now that you're preparing to move forward into the test content chapters of this book, be sure to keep your goal in mind. As you read, think about how you will be able to apply this information on the test. If you've already seen sample questions for the test and you have an idea of the question format and style, try to come up with questions of your own that you can answer based on what you're reading. This will give you valuable practice applying your knowledge in the same ways you can expect to on test day.

Good luck and good studying!

External Financial Reporting Decisions

Balance Sheet

The balance sheet is also called the statement of financial position or the statement of condition. It is a snapshot of the assets, liabilities, and owners' equity of an organization at a given point in time. The purpose of the balance sheet is to show what the organization owns (its assets), what it owes (its liabilities), and the investment made by shareholders (its shareholder equity). The balance sheet follows a specific formula where assets equal liabilities plus shareholders' equity. The balance in these categories happens because the organization pays for its assets by either borrowing money (taking out a liability) or raising funds from shareholders (adding to shareholder equity). There are many accounts within the categories of assets, liabilities, and shareholders' equity. The account listing within each category varies from organization to organization.

Balance Sheet Purpose

The balance sheet is used by investors, shareholders, creditors, and other decision makers to determine the makeup of an organization's resources, its dependence on external financing, and its ability to be flexible and adapt to new business conditions. In addition, an organization's management can use the balance sheet to further understand the operations of the organization. A study of the assets and liabilities can reveal the strength of the organization's short-term financial position. In a financially strong organization, assets should be double the amount of liabilities. By comparing balance sheets for different operating periods, trends in operations can be discovered, strengths and weaknesses can be determined, and problems and opportunities can be uncovered. The balance sheet can give a picture of the organization's financial position. It can show if the assets are being used profitably, if inventory is being turned over at an appropriate rate, and how much leverage the organization uses compared to its competitors. Also, the balance sheet is the primary financial statement that lenders, investors, and clients request of an organization.

Balance Sheet Contents

A balance sheet contains three categories of accounts – assets, liabilities, and shareholders' equity. Assets are the financial resources available to the organization such as cash, accounts receivable, deposits, inventory, property, patents, and equipment. Assets may be either fully paid for or there may be a debt obligation associated with the asset. Assets are broken down into current assets and fixed assets. Current assets are those assets that can easily be turned into cash. Current assets are liquid. Fixed assets are those assets that the organization expects to retain for a long period of time. Liabilities are the external loans of the organization and include accounts payable, accrued expenses, taxes payable, short-term loans, mortgages, and long-term loans. Liabilities are broken down into short-term liabilities and long-term liabilities. The shareholders' equity is the difference between assets and liabilities. It is equal to the shareholders' contributions (in the form of shares of stock) and the earnings retained by the organization. The shareholder's equity is the net worth of the company.

Working Capital

Working capital is a measure of an organization's operating capital. It is calculated by subtracting current liabilities from current assets. When there is a positive working capital, that is, current assets are higher than current liabilities; an organization is liquid and will have no problems paying off their short-term liabilities. When there is negative working capital, it means that the organization will not be able to meet its short-term liabilities. Working capital can be used to determine the efficiency at which the organization operates. Examples of efficiency are the ability to collect on accounts receivable and the control of the amount of cash tied up in inventory.

Income Statement

Contents

An income statement contains revenues, expenses, gains, losses, discontinued operations, extraordinary gains and losses, accounting changes, and net income. Revenues are cash amounts received from an organization's operations. Revenues may include sales income, interest income, and rental income. Expenses are cash amounts paid from activities that relate to an organization's operations. Expenses may include cost of goods sold, salaries paid, interest paid on debt, and materials purchased. Gains are increases in assets that are not due to the organization's everyday operations. Gains may come from the sale of property or the early payment of a debt. Losses are decreases in assets that are not due to the organization's everyday operations. Losses may be incurred when investments are sold or from a lawsuit. Discontinued operations occur when an organization sells, abandons, or disposes of a part of its business. Extraordinary gains and losses are events that are unusual for the organization and occur infrequently. Extraordinary gains and losses occur because of a major casualty, property seizure, or a regulatory change. Accounting changes are changes in accounting principles, accounting estimates, or the reporting entity.

Income Statement Definition

The income statement is also called the statement of profit and loss, the statement of earnings, or the statement of operations. The income statement details the earnings of the organization for a given period. This is done by summarizing the revenues and expenses for the period and calculating the profit or loss for that period. The income statement provides a picture of the organization's performance from operations. Income statements are prepared on an accrual basis or a cash basis. In an accrual system, income and expenses are recorded when they are incurred. In a cash system, income and expenses are recorded when they are paid. Income statements are used to determine the past performance of an organization, predict future performance, and determine the risk of realizing future cash flows. The disadvantages of the income statement are that intangible assets (such as goodwill and brand loyalty) cannot be measured, financial figures can be reported differently based on the accounting method used, and financial figures are dependent on judgment and speculation (such as depreciation).

Purpose

The income statement contains information to compute return on investment, risk, financial flexibility, and operating capabilities. The return on investment measures the organization's performance. Risk measures the uncertainty of the organization's future. Financial flexibility measures the organization's ability to make changes when there are problems or opportunities. Operating capability is a measure of an organization's ability to maintain a specified operating level. The income statement is also used to estimate the amount, timing, and uncertainty of future cash flows. Investors, creditors, and financial analysts use income statements to determine an organization's future profitability. Also included in the income statement is the calculation of earnings per share. The earnings per share figure is calculated by dividing the net income by the number of outstanding shares of common stock. The income statement is the most analyzed financial statement. The income statement indicates how successful an organization will be based on its earnings from operations.

Structure

Included in the income statement are revenues and expenses incurred as a result of the organization's daily activities. The income statement takes sales and subtracts the cost of sales to come up with the gross margin. Operating expenses are deducted from the gross margin to determine income from operations. Then, other income and expenses are added or subtracted to show the income before taxes. The provision for incomes taxes is deducted to figure the income from continuing operations. Transactions that are outside the normal course of business are detailed at the end of the income statement after the accounting for taxes. These irregular transactions include discontinued operations, accounting changes, and extraordinary items. The net income figure is shown at the bottom of the income statement.

STATEMENT OF CASH FLOWS

The statement of cash flows is a quarterly statement that a publicly traded company is required to submit to the SEC and its shareholders. The statement of cash flows includes information about the cash an organization receives from operations and investments, and the cash an organization pays out for business activities and investments. The reason for the statement of cash flows is because many organizations use the accrual method of accounting. The accrual method does not represent the actual cash received and spent by the organization, only the obligations due to it and incurred by it. The accrual method does not represent a real picture of an organization's profitability. It may represent an inflated level of profitability if the accrued revenue is never actually received. The statement of cash flows shows if an organization is having a cash flow problem and therefore a problem meeting its financial obligations.

STATEMENT OF CASH FLOWS PURPOSE

The statement of cash flows is used by creditors and investors. These individuals look at the statement of cash flows to determine if the organization will be able to meet its debt and dividend payments. The statement of cash flows categorizes the sources and uses of cash to show the amount of cash an organization generates and uses in its operations. The statement of cash flows lists the amount of money that was spent for items that do not appear on the income statement. These items may include debt repayments, the purchase of a fixed asset, and dividend payments. In 1987, the statement of cash flows replaced the statement of changes in financial position as a required financial statement.

CONTENTS

The statement of cash flows is a report on the cash receipts and cash payments of the organization. These cash flow amounts are classified according to operating activities, investing activities, and financing activities. The operating, investing, and financing amounts are then reconciled to the net income for the accounting period. Operating activities include cash received from the sale of products and services, and payments made for products and services used in the course of conducting business. Investing activities are the purchase of property, plant, equipment, and other assets needed to conduct and grow the business. Financing activities include those amounts that are put into the organization by shareholders or amounts borrowed by the organization.

STATEMENT OF CHANGES IN SHAREHOLDERS' EQUITY

The statement of changes in shareholders' equity shows changes in the equity position of the organization over a specified period of time. The equity items that are shown include investments by shareholders, capital contributions, earnings for the period, and distributions to shareholders (also known as dividends). If an organization does not provide a statement of changes in shareholders' equity, it may provide a statement of changes in retained earnings. The statement of changes in retained earnings is also called the statement of earned surplus. The statement of changes in retained earnings shows how net income and dividends paid for the period changed from the beginning of the period to the end of the period. The changes in contributed capital are detailed on the balance sheet or on the notes to the balance sheet.

Notes to the Financial Statements

The notes to the financial statements contain information regarding the data contained in the financial statements. These notes are usually added to the end of the appropriate financial statement. Information contained in the notes can include a variety of information. The organization may need to explain circumstances regarding debt financing and repayment. If there are going concern issues, this will need to be explained. Going concern refers to an organization's ability to earn sufficient income to continue operations. Accountants may also add notes to the financial statements when a disclosure about the financial information needs to be made. Contingent liabilities that may or may not be incurred by the organization in the future need to be disclosed in the notes to the financial statements. Contingent liabilities depend on the outcome of some event, such as a lawsuit.

Direct Method and Indirect Method for Creating a Statement of Cash Flows

The direct method for creating a statement of cash flows uses cash receipts and cash payments to calculate the cash flow. It starts by adding money received from loans and sales. From this amount, expenses, capital expenditures, loan repayments, and taxes are deducted. The indirect method for creating a statement of cash flows uses net income as the starting point of the cash flow calculation. Deducted from net income are the transactions for all non-cash transactions. Non-cash transactions include depreciation, changes in accounts receivable, changes in liabilities, capital expenditures, investments, dividends, stock purchases and sales, and changes in debt.

Integrated Reporting

Integrated reporting provides a "big picture" overview of a company's overall performance. It reveals how a company creates and sustains its value based on a variety of factors that reach beyond the traditional financial statement. Integrated reporting starts with the theory that when a company's strategy creates sustainable value, it impacts its overall performance and market value.

Integrated reporting is designed to display the interdependencies between a company's strategy, operations, present opportunities, risk management, social impact, environmental footprint, and financial reporting to give stakeholders an overall view of the company's short-term and long-term value. Realizing the connection between the internal and external factors and their impact on the overall creation of value will allow a company to take an integrated approach to its decision-making, as opposed to a departmental view. Integrated reporting gives the company the tools that it needs to strategically manage operations and mitigate risks that could impact their sustainability over time.

International Accounting Standards Board (IASB)

The IASB was founded on April 1, 2001 to serve as an independent standard-setting committee for the IFRS Foundation. The IASB works toward the global convergence of accounting standards by cultivating and implementing International Financial Reporting Standards (IFRS). They also desire to assess the needs for financial reporting which arise from developing economies and small and medium-sized entities (SMEs).

The board was originally created with fifteen members, but the trustees of the IASB voted in January 2009 to expand the number of members in the IASB to sixteen by July 2012. According to the IFRS website (www.ifrs.org), the terms of the board members begin and end at various dates and persist for various durations, but through the site one can easily learn who the current board members are. The board members display a range of national diversity, ranging from America to the UK, the Netherlands, Sweden, Germany, France, Brazil, South Africa, India, South Korea, Japan, and China.

Governmental Accounting Standards Board (GASB)

Despite its name, the GASB is not a governmental body, but is rather a private-sector board, formed in 1984 as a section of the Financial Accounting Foundation (FAF), whose objective is to form and enhance accounting standards for state and local governments in the U.S. Due to the differences between for-profit accounting and governmental accounting, it is important that a separate standard-setting body be erected to clarify the relevant issues and provide clear standards. The GASB's declarations are recognized as the authoritative standards of generally accepted accounting principles (GAAP) for state and local governmental accounting.

Asset Valuation

Asset valuation is the method determining the worth of something such as a company, real property, a security, or other item of value. An asset valuation is usually performed prior to the sale of an asset or prior to purchasing insurance for the asset. It can include both objective and subjective measurements. There are objective measurements such as the net profit of a company or the stock price of a company. On the other hand, something like brand name recognition has no measurable value and is thus subjective.

Valuation of Liabilities

The value of a liability is generally known, but occasionally it must be estimated. A liability is usually valued on the balance sheet as either the amount of money needed to pay a debt or the fair market value of goods or services to be delivered.

Revenue Recognition

Revenue Recognition – Income is reported when earned, regardless of when the payment is received. This is usually denoted when the two following conditions are satisfied:

1. Earnings process is or nearly is complete.

- Revenues are recognized at time of exchange, e.g., sale, percentage of completion, production, installments, or cost recovery basis.

Planning, Budgeting and Forecasting

Budgeting

Importance

Budgets are the major tool used by organizations to help plan the business finances and achieve financial success. The budget outlines the financial plan of the organization and determines the actions to be taken to acquire and use resources. Budgets set goals and standards for sales revenue, employee staffing, inventory levels, investments and borrowing, and capital expenditures. These goals and standards are used by management when implementing projects and give management guidance for the execution of projects. Budgets are also used as benchmarks that the organization can use to compare expected results against actual results. When the expected results do not meet actual results, budgets can give an indication of the corrective action that needs to be taken to meet the goals.

Purpose

A budget is an estimate of what an organization expects to earn and spend during a specified period of time. Future budgets are usually based on past financial records and adjusted to reflect proposed changes and economic conditions. These predicted amounts are only expected to act as a guideline and are reevaluated on a periodic basis. A budget gives an organization financial numbers to use so that business plans can be formulated and goals can be met. Budgets help with planning business operations, communicating organizational goals, organizing work within the organization, and maintaining organizational control.

Timeline

The budgeting process is governed by the budget planning calendar. This is a schedule of all of the activities that need to be accomplished in order to develop and approve a budget. The budget planning calendar divides the parts of the master budget among the responsible departments. The most important part of the budget planning calendar is the dates on which each individual or department is to provide information pertaining to the budget.

Guidelines Needed to Create an Accurate Budget

Budget guidelines are needed to minimize slacks and abuses in the budget amounts. Budgets should not contain amounts that are more than what is actually needed to meet the organization's goals. When budget amounts are inflated, a department will seem to have performed in excess of expectations. When budget amounts are lower than what is actually needed, it may have a discouraging effect on employees and employee morale. In addition, management must take the budget seriously so that the organization's employees realize that the budget is an important part of their job performance and expectations.

Process

The budget process is the method in which a budget is created and approved. The budget process is started in the financial department of an organization where the prior year financial figures are distributed to the various departments within the organization. Each department then compares the prior year figures to projected plans and formulates the amount of money that will be earned and spent on the projected plans. These projected budgets are then either adjusted or approved by executive management.

Importance of Control

Budget controls are those budgetary actions that must be carried out in accordance with the budget plan. This control ensures that an organization's budget is effective in implementing its plans and objectives.

Communication Tool

Budgets are the main tool used by organizations to turn plans into action oriented goals and objectives. When budgetary guidelines are followed, it is more likely that goals and objectives can be achieved. The budget is an important tool in communicating the operational results expected by the organization and how the members of the organization can achieve these results. Budgets provide each manager and department with the expected income to be achieved and the costs that can be incurred. The budget communicates each manager's and department's accountability for the transactions and tasks under their influence and control. The budget gives benchmark figures so that the success or failure at meeting goals can be evaluated. The budget shows where each manager and department deviated from the plan.

Effective Elements

An effective budget uses historical financial data as the base of the budget and incorporates planned and anticipated costs and revenues to forecast the organization's financial needs. It requires that management have an in-depth knowledge and understanding of the factors that affect and influence the organization.

Authoritative Budgeting Process

The authoritative budgeting process is a top-down approach to setting organizational goals and determining budget figures. In the authoritative budgeting process, upper level management sets the parameters under which the budget is prepared. The parameters may include sales goals, cost levels, or compensation levels. Upper level management is also the final authority in determining budget figures. In the authoritative budget method, employees that are affected by the budget and who are expected to meet budget goals do not provide any information about the anticipated costs and income from their departments. The only role that employees play is in calculating budget figures based on the parameters set by upper level management. The figures obtained for the authoritative budget are derived from historical accounting data and from management's expectations.

Advantages and Disadvantages of the Authoritative Budgeting Process

There are several advantages to the authoritative budgeting process. The authoritative budgeting process allows upper level management to determine the level at which the organization should operate. It gives upper level management the ability to set sales and production goals. It allows upper level management to make the organizational goals known to employees in the most efficient manner. In addition, it is quicker to put together a budget using the authoritative method because the input comes from a limited number of individuals. There are also several disadvantages to the authoritative budget. The authoritative budgeting process may be seen as dictatorial and may result in moral and resentment problems. This may result in lower level managers and employees not being committed to meeting organizational goals and budget figures. Another disadvantage is that the budget figures may be unrealistic and unattainable.

The budgeting process involves teamwork between the departments within an organization. This teamwork is enhanced as the budget is compiled with employee participation working from the bottom up to management. When accomplished this way, departments are given an opportunity to express what they need and require in order to achieve the organization's goals. In this system, management should set guidelines and parameters in which the budget figures should be developed. When employees are given a say in the budget process, they will work to achieve or exceed budget expectations.

Participative Budgeting Process

The participative budgeting process is a budgeting method that gives employees the opportunity to provide input into the budgeting process. In the participative budget method, those employees that are affected by the budget provide information about the anticipated costs and income from their department. The input from employees can result in budget figures that are realistic and attainable. Participative budgets are used as a motivation tool. When employees are involved in the process and allowed to give input, they are more likely to accomplish the work needed to meet or exceed budget goals. The employees are motivated to cooperate with each other. The participative budgeting process gives employees a sense of ownership in the outcome and output of the organization. When employees have this type of input, they are able to make the connection between their performance and the performance of the organization.

Disadvantages of Participative Budgeting

The participative budgeting process is a time consuming process because it involves employees at every level within an organization. It takes time to collect information from a large number of individuals, to process the information gathered, to evaluate the input from many sources, and to compile that collected data into a single budget. In addition to requiring an investment in time, the participative budgeting process requires an investment of money and resources to implement. Instead of performing their daily jobs, employees spend time on the budgeting process. This results in a loss of income and productivity. The participative budgeting process may result in budget figures that are unrealistic. Managers and employees may inflate costs if they feel management will not give them the budget they want or need. On the other hand, budget figures may be underestimated in order to make it easier to achieve budget goals.

Budgetary Slack

Budgetary slack occurs when income is underestimated and/or costs are overestimated in a budget. When creating a budget, there may be a tendency to set sales goals that are lower than what can be attained or to set costs that are higher than needed. This may be done to make is easier to attain the budget goals and gain higher performance evaluations. When budget goals are low, it is easier to exceed the budget goals. This results in an unrealistic increase in performance but does not result in advancing the organizational goals. Budgetary slack does not provide any incentive for employees to actually increase their performance. Once they have met the unrealistically low budget goals, there is a tendency to reduce performance. Sales will not be maximized and costs will not be minimized. This ensures that the same budgetary slack will be incorporated into future budgets. Budgetary slack also encourages waste. Management may overspend so that budget amounts will not be reduced in future budget periods.

Zero-Based Budgeting

Zero-based budgeting is a budgeting method where budget figures are not based on prior performance. For each budget period, the budget figures are determined based on the goals of the organization and past performance is not taken into consideration. Zero-based budgeting focuses on efficiency and only those budget figures that are necessary to achieve future goals are taken into consideration. By using the zero-based budgeting method, inefficiency is kept to a minimum and budgetary slack is also kept to a minimum. A disadvantage of zero-based budgeting is that it is time consuming and expensive to implement. This added cost must be balanced against the reduction in efficiency and budgetary slack. It is not necessary to use zero-based budgeting every year to reduce the occurrence of budgetary slack. Zero-based budgeting can be effective at reducing budgetary slack if implemented in one out of every 3 or 4 years of the budget cycle.

Purpose of Setting Standards

Standards are the budgeted unit costs that are used to produce an optimal level of productivity and efficiency. The purpose is to indicate when actual costs are different than budgeted or standard costs. The standard cost system is used in conjunction with flexible budgeting methods. By using flexible budgeting, an organization can prepare different budgets for different production levels and it can determine the different costs for each of those production levels. Costs at different production levels will be different because of economies of scale. When actual costs are different than standard costs, there is a variance. When there is a variance, it is important to identify the reason for the variance and to assign responsibility for the variance. This allows management to collect information that will lead to a solution and to provide for continuous improvement in the manufacturing process. In addition, information about the cause of the variance is also useful in evaluating management's performance.

Practical Standards

Practical standards are also called currently attainable standards. Practical standards set a performance level that can be reasonably achieved and also allow for normal waste, spoilage, and downtime. Practical standards are not necessarily easy to achieve; it is possible to achieve practical standards but it may be difficult to achieve the expected results. When using practical standards, standard costs must be kept current to avoid a variance. When standard costs are not kept current for budgeting purposes, the usefulness of the budget is diminished because of the variance that occurs. The purpose of the variance is to indicate that an unusual event has happened.

Ideal Standards

Ideal standards are also called perfection, theoretical, or maximum efficiency standards. Ideal standards set the basis for what costs should be when production is operating under optimal conditions. Ideal standards assume that the most skilled workers are being utilized and there is no allowance for waste, spoilage, or downtime. Ideal standards can have positive and negative effects on worker motivation. Ideal standards may motivate employees to perform at their highest potential. If the ideal standards are difficult to achieve, there will be a negative effect on employee morale. Ideal standards are most often used by organizations that have adopted continuous improvement or total quality management principles and procedures. Ideal standards are not used in budgets that require financial planning such as cash budgeting, product costing, and departmental performance budgeting.

Impact of Unattainable Budget Standards

Unattainable budget standards occur when management sets budget goals that cannot be realistically attained. Budget goals may be unrealistic when sales goals are set higher than what the current customer base will purchase or when costs are set so low that it is not possible to manufacture a product at those costs. When budget goals are unrealistic, employees will not be able to achieve the standards set by management. This may cause employees to become frustrated and disenchanted which in turn will create poor performance results and reduce the morale level. Once management sets unattainable budget standards, the following year's budget goals may not be followed by employees. The employees may lose confidence in management's ability to accurately and fairly estimate attainable sales goals and reasonable costs of production.

Purpose of Controllable Costs in the Budgeting Process

Controllable costs are the variable costs that can be influenced by an organization. These variable costs include materials, labor, and product-related overhead. Some fixed costs are also considered controllable costs. These costs include expenses that relate to a specific product or department within the organization.

Operational or Operating Budget

An operational budget is used to make operating decisions for an organization. It is a forecast of sales, income, cost of goods sold, and expenses. The operational budget is a compilation of all of the different types of budgets that an organization will need to produce in order to ensure successful operations. In order to prepare an operational budget, an organization will first need to prepare the sales, production, ending inventory, direct material, direct labor, factory overhead, selling, and administrative budgets. The operational budget gives an organization an estimate of the resources it will need in order to meet its goals.

Effects of Unattainable Budget Standards

When upper level management sets budget goals that are unattainable, it may lead to financial reporting that is inaccurate or misleading. This inaccurate financial reporting is used to deceive upper level management so that temporary problems in meeting the unrealistic goals are not detected. Even though the reporting error may be minor, over time the problem could escalate until it leads to significant financial difficulties for the organization. To avoid these problems, upper level management must set budget standards that are realistic and attainable. In addition, lower level management must report difficulties in achieving performance goals. This two-way communication is necessary to avoid the financial difficulties and possible collapse of the organization that can occur when budget standards are not adhered to.

Purpose of a Capital Expenditure Budget

A capital expenditure budget is used to plan for capital expenditure projects. Capital expenditure projects involve making a capital investment in facilities and equipment, research and development of new products, or paying off long-term debt. The capital expenditure budget shows when assets need to be replaced, the cost of acquiring assets, and construction costs of facilities and equipment. The capital expenditure budget is used to determine whether or not a capital project should be pursued.

Regression Analysis

Regression analysis is a statistical method that measures the relationship between a dependent variable and one or more other variables that change value. Regression analysis Regression analysis is used to measure how much a changing variable, such as interest rates, affect the price of another variable, such as a financial investment. Trends can also be predicted with regression analysis. By measuring the historical changes of the independent variables in relation to the dependent variable, the future value of the dependent variable can be predicted.

Multiple Regression

Multiple regression is a method of dealing with relationships between variables. It measures the changes in one variable that are associated with changes in two or more other variables. For example, multiple regression can measure the changes in sales that are associated with changes in demographic data.

Simple (or Linear) Regression

Linear regression is a method of dealing with relationships between variables. Linear regression measures the expected value of a variable based on the values of another variable. Linear regression is used for capital asset pricing and for determining the potential return on risky assets.

Learning Curve

A learning curve is a graphical depiction that shows the efficiencies gained from experience. It shows the relationship between the number of units produced and the time spent per unit. The basic theory is that the cost per unit of output goes down as learning and experience are gained. When an individual first learns a new task, they are high on the learning curve. This means that the cost per unit is high and output is low. As an individual learns a task, they move down the learning curve. They become more efficient. They are less hesitant, make fewer mistakes, learn to automate, and make adjustments to the way they perform a task. Learning curve analysis is used to make pricing decisions, schedule labor and other production resources, develop capital budgets, and set wage rates.

Annual or Master Budget

The annual budget outlines the plans of an organization for its fiscal year. The purpose of the annual budget is to control the day to day operations of the organization. The annual budget also sets priorities for accomplishing the long-term goals of the organization by allocating resources to each of the activities outlined in the organization's strategic plan. The annual budget is a compilation of the budgets of each individual department.

Project Budgeting

Project budgeting is the method an organization uses to allocate money and resources to an individual project. The project budget details the money and other resources needed to construct new facilities, acquire land, purchase equipment, finance expansion, and pay for professional services.

Creating an Annual or Master Budget

The first budget to be created is the sales budget. This gives the organization an estimate of the materials needed to meet these sales figures. Next is the production budget. This will give the organization an estimate of the materials and labor needed to meet the sales goals. Then there is the cash budget. This will determine if the organization will generate enough cash during the budget period to meet its financial needs and whether or not financing will be needed during the budget period. The last item to be created is the forecasted balance sheet. The forecasted balance sheet consists of cash balances, accounts receivable, investments, inventory, accounts payable, wages payable, taxes payable, and equity. The forecasted balance sheet ensures that assets equal liabilities.

Zero Based Budgeting

Zero based budgeting is a method that requires that budgeted figures be justified for each new budget period. In other budgeting methods, only the amount needed in excess of the prior period's budgeted amounts needs to be explained and justified. Zero based budgeting requires that the budget figures show how the dollar amounts projected will attain the goals of the organization.

Activity Based Budgeting

Activity based budgeting is the process of creating a budget based on activities and not on costs. It is a way to allocate resources among the various activities and business process of an organization.

The activity based budget is a forecast of the labor and financial resources needed to achieve an organization's goals.

Kaizen Budgeting

Kaizen budgeting is a budgeting method that looks for continuous improvement in the budgeting process. During this process, each aspect of the budget process is looked at and evaluated. Any changes that could create improvement are then incorporated into the next budgeting cycle.

Continuous Budget

A continuous budget is one that is always provides a forecast for a future 12 month period. Most budgets only provide a forecast for the current fiscal period. A continuous budget is updated each month so that an organization can always see its budget predications 12 months in advance. This allows the organization to have a budget that remains current and relevant.

Static Budget and Flexible Budget Differences

A static budget forecasts one level of production results for the budget period and the costs associated with the projected production level. On the other hand, a flexible budget projects revenues and costs for several production levels. When budget figures are not reached, a flexible budget is more useful than a static budget because the flexible budget allows management to look at the variances between the budget and the actual results in better detail which in turn gives a better indication of performance and ways to improve performance. The flexible budget allows management to change performance plans during a budget period and to determine the effect those changes will have on the financial condition of the organization. The other advantage of the flexible budget is that it allows management to compare the actual costs with the projected costs for the actual production level. This gives the organization greater control over costs.

Flexible Budgeting

Flexible budgeting allows for modifications to be made in the budget to the actual level of performance. For example, if a budget is set for a production of 100 units but the actual production is 200 units, the budget will be adjusted to show budgeted (but not actual) revenues and costs for 200 units produced at the per unit price of the 100 units. Flexible budgeting gives more meaningful information and provides a basis for comparison.

Sales Budget

The sales budget is an operating plan that shows forecasted sales volume and the sales price of each product produced by an organization. The sales budget is one of the first budgets that should be developed in the budgeting process. The sales budget projects sales volume and sales volume is an important factor in determining all of the other figures that need to be forecasted in the budgeting process.

Purpose of the Annual Profit Plan

The purpose of the annual profit plan is to help create an annual or master budget. The annual profit plan is a forecast of the revenues and expenses of an organization and computes the net income or net loss to the organization for the budget period. The annual profit plan consists of performing what-if analysis on various project scenarios that an organization may undertake during the budget period.

Production Budget

The production budget is an estimate of the amount of product an organization will need to produce during the budget period. The production budget uses the sales budget and forecasted inventory levels to determine the production budget. The production budget includes forecasts for material, labor, and manufacturing costs. Material and labor are an identifiable part of the finished product. Manufacturing costs include equipment depreciation, utilities, and production management.

Costs Detailed in the Production Budget

The production budget consists of overhead costs that are directly related to manufacturing. These costs include manufacturing supplies used in the production process, supervisor salaries, factory maintenance, equipment repair, and utilities.

Sales Forecast

A sales forecast is a prediction of sales volume for a future period. It is a necessary component of the annual or master budget. The sales forecast is the basis for planning production capacity, production levels, inventory quantities, labor requirements, and purchasing amounts. Sales forecasting can be accomplished by either qualitative or quantitative approaches. Qualitative approaches include surveys of sales personnel and consumers. Quantitative methods include mathematical models such as moving average, exponential smoothing, trend analysis, and regression analysis.

Direct Material Budget

The direct material budget is a component of the production budget and divides the production process into its basic components. It indicates the amount of material needed for production. The direct material budget also forecasts the amount of inventory and material needed in order to meet the organization's goals.

Overhead Budget

The overhead budget is the expected costs that may be incurred in the manufacturing process. It does not include direct material and direct labor costs. The overhead budget does include indirect material, indirect labor, rent, and insurance. Overhead budget amounts include variable costs, fixed costs, and a combination of fixed and variable costs.

Determining Accurate Overhead Expenses

Overhead expenses are important in the calculation of cost of goods sold and in setting a profitable sales price for products. In the budgeting process, these exact costs are not known and must be estimated. During the budgeting process, these overhead expenses can be estimated by projecting sales volume, production volume, and production costs. Activity bases can be used to determine the percentage of overhead costs to be applied to each product. These activity bases include direct labor hours, direct labor costs, machine hours, sales dollar, gross margin dollars, and employee count.

Components of Overhead Expense

Overhead expenses are those production and non-production costs that cannot be linked to a particular job or department. Production overhead expenses consist of indirect material, indirect labor, taxes, insurance, depreciation, utilities, and maintenance. Non-production overhead costs include maintenance personnel salaries, plant and equipment insurance, regulatory costs, and administrative expenses.

Direct Labor Budget

The direct labor budget is an estimate of the workforce needed to meet the organization's production schedule and output. This estimate is computed based on the production volume specified in the production budget. To compile a direct labor budget, the organization will need to use industrial engineering guidelines and production needs to forecast labor requirements. The budget figure is determined by multiplying the production volume by the direct labor hours per unit of production. This figure is then multiplied by the direct labor cost per hour to come up with the direct labor costs.

Selling and Administrative Budget

The selling and administrative budget is an estimate of those costs that will be incurred on behalf of the sales and operations departments of an organization. These costs include marketing and advertising costs, sales commissions, distribution costs, management salaries, administrative staff salaries, office rent, legal and accounting fees, and other office expenses.

Cash Budget

The cash budget determines whether or not an organization will need to borrow funds or pursue some other financing means in order to meet its cash flow needs. The cash budget is determined by taking the cash available at the beginning of the budget period, adding sources of cash (such as receivables and sales), and subtracting cash disbursements (such as payables and material purchases). If the amount is negative, an organization will need to look at financing alternatives. If the amount is positive, an organization can look at investment opportunities.

Elements of a Cash Budget

The cash budget contains four sections—receipts, disbursements, cash surplus or deficit, and financing. The receipts section contains the beginning cash balance, expected accounts receivables collected from customers, and all other anticipated cash receipts. The disbursements section includes all projected cash payments to be made organized by the type of payment. The cash surplus or deficit section is the difference between the cash receipts and the disbursements. The financing section details the loans expected to be taken out and loan amounts expected to be repaid during the budget period.

Purpose of the Budget for Acquisition of Capital Assets

The budget for acquisition of capital assets is a planning method for the purchase and replacement of long-term assets. It includes financing methods for these assets. This budget is developed using capital budgeting techniques such as the payback method, the net present value method, and the internal rate of return method.

Purpose of a Pro Forma Statement of Financial Position

The pro forma statement of financial position is a projected balance sheet. It is used to determine how an organization will be utilizing its assets in the future. The pro forma statement of financial position shows how much of the assets are projected to be used by accounts receivables, inventory, and equipment.

Developing a Pro Forma Income Statement

The first step toward creating a pro forma income statement is to look at the current income statement and determine which items will change in the predicted period. First expected cost of goods sold is subtracted from expected sales to determine the pro forma gross profit. Then, expected expenses are determined and subtracted from pro forma gross profit to come up with pro forma profit before taxes. Finally, expected taxes are determined and subtracted from pro form profit before taxes to come up with pro forma profit after taxes.

Purpose of a Pro Forma Cash Flow Statement

A pro forma cash flow statement is used to predict an organization's income and spending. It helps an organization determine if it will have a cash shortage during the predicted period so that measures can be taken to cover the cash shortages. Cash shortages can be covered by taking out a loan, selling capital stock, seeking higher sales, or reducing expenses.

Developing a Pro Forma Statement of Financial Position

To create a pro forma statement of financial position, each item on the balance sheet must be projected for the budget period. Cash is estimated using a cash flow projection. Accounts receivable are estimated using average collection time and sales projections. Projected cash and projected accounts receivable are added to come up with pro forma total current assets. Pro forma fixed assets are calculated by taking the value of the assets and subtracting depreciation. Pro forma current liabilities are the amounts that will be spent on supplies, payroll, and loans. Pro forma owners' equity is pro forma total liabilities subtracted from pro forma total assets.

Developing a Pro Forma Cash Flow Statement

Before a pro forma cash flow statement can be compiled, the organization will need to determine its present cash position. Then, all sources of future cash inflows will need to be listed. These sources of cash income include accounts receivables from prior period's sales and sales made and paid for during the current period. Next, all uses of future cash must be listed. This includes cost of goods sold, operating expenses, and income taxes. The cash uses are subtracted from the cash sources to determine the net change in cash position. Finally, the net change in cash position is added to the starting cash figure to give the starting cash figure for the pro forma cash flow period.

Purpose of a Pro Forma Income Statement

A pro forma income statement is a tool used to plan future business operations. It helps an organization make changes in its operations based on future predicted profitability. If an organization determines that profitability may go down, it can make changes such as increasing prices or decreasing costs to avoid potential losses. A pro forma income statement is also used to predict the level of sales and expenses during different time periods within the budget period. This can help an organization determine whether or not sales efforts must be increased during a certain portion of the year.

Significance of a Company's Mission and Objectives

The mission of a company is the purpose for the company's very existence. It can generally be captured in a mission statement, articulating how the company differs from others and defining the extent of the company's products and customer base. A mission statement sometimes includes what the company seeks to become in the future; if this statement is separate, it can be called a "vision statement." Mission statements and vision statements can be as broad or as narrow as needed. Objectives provide a specified quantity and deadline as part of the company's strategy. Because of the quantifiable nature of objectives, they are sometimes distinguished from goals, which are broader or unquantified statements of a company's pursuits.

Integrated Business Planning (IBP)

Integrated business planning (IBP) seeks to holistically provide a model for a company, interrelating its different functions and organizational segments in order to maximize the use of technology and to link different forms of planning (operational, strategic, and financial planning). IBP helps companies to maximize efficiency and provides them a competitive advantage by explicating the relations among the different facets of the company.

Basics of Performance Measures

Due to the many different facets of an organization's performance, it can be difficult to accurately measure. A company's financial statements can help to show its financial position for a given time or time span, but scorecards can help to better measure non-financial features. Scorecards may require additional judgment and effort to create, since they need to be specifically helpful for a particular industry or company and therefore could mislead a company for which the scorecard is not intended. Moreover, the preparation of scorecards is not a strictly scientific process, but requires judgment which is not standardized or codified. Balanced scorecards should seek to answer information concerning the business's customers, innovation, strategies, and financial information.

Regression Analysis, the Coefficient of Correlation, and the Coefficient of Determination Aid in Forecasting

Regression analysis seeks to discern a quantifiable relationship between some dependent variable and some independent variable(s), although it does not necessarily establish a causal relationship between or among them. Simple regression analysis analyzes a dependent variable in relation to one independent variable, whereas multiple regression analysis analyzes a dependent variable in relation to at least two independent variables. The coefficient of correlation (R) calculates the degree to which a dependent variable and a single independent variable are linearly related. A value of 1 or -1 signifies a perfectly linear relationship between the two—i.e. all the (x,y) points for the two variables form a perfectly straight line—whereas a value of 0 signifies that no linear relation at all exists between them; the (x,y) points for the variables would be a pure scatterplot. The values for R must fall between 1 and -1. The coefficient of determination is the square of the coefficient of correlation, and so can also be represented as R^2. It therefore must lie between 0 and 1. The closer R^2 is to 1, the more we can be sure that independent variable is responsible for whatever variability there is with the dependent variable.

Forecasting and the Delphi Technique

Forecasting is an effort to predict future events. Forecasting can be done using either qualitative methods or quantitative methods. Qualitative methods are subjective and rely on management's judgment, opinion, and expertise to develop a prediction for the future. Qualitative methods may include getting opinions from within the organization, such as management or employees. Qualitative methods may include surveys from customers and the Delphi technique.

The Delphi technique uses expert opinion to make forecasts through a group consensus. Advantages of the Delphi technique include the following:

1. It is a rapid and efficient way to gain objective information from a group of experts.
2. It involves less effort for a respondent to answer a well-designed questionnaire than to participate in a conference or write a paper.
3. It can be highly motivating for a group of experts to see the responses of knowledgeable persons.
4. The use of systematic procedures applies an air of objectivity to the outcomes.
5. The results of Delphi exercises are subject to greater acceptance on the part of the group.

A disadvantage of the Delphi technique is that each trend is given unilateral consideration on its own merits.

Performance Management

Performance Measurement

Performance measurement is the use of statistics to measure the progress an organization has made in meeting its goals and objectives. The purpose of performance measurement is to determine progress so that improvement can be made if necessary. This process starts with measuring data and providing feedback so that the management and staff of an organization can take corrective action to improve performance. There are many challenges when performing performance measurements. One challenge is the range of skills involved when dealing with a large staff. When each staff member performs a different task, it is difficult to come up with a uniform measurement that will rate each staff member equally. Performance measurement methods do not take the contribution of intangible assets into account. These intangible assets can only be evaluated based on non-financial measurements which are based on judgment and experience.

Performance Evaluation Measures

Performance measurement is an indication of an organization's effectiveness and efficiency in conducting business operations. The performance evaluation measurers that are used include revenue center, cost center, profit center, and investment center. The revenue center measurement compares actual revenue for a period with the expected revenue for that same period. The cost center measurement compares actual costs for a period with expected costs for that period. The profit center measurement looks at the revenues and costs incurred in determining net income. The investment center measurement looks at the revenues and costs that comprise net income for the period and also takes into account the investments that contributed to net income. Investment center measurements are calculated using return on investment and residual income formulas.

Measuring Performance Basic Guidelines

The performance measurement process should involve process improvement, employee participation, reporting requirements, future planning, total organization improvement, realistic goals, and management commitment. Process improvement means that management and staff should be aware of the purpose of performance measurement and how this purpose will meet organizational goals. It also means that the performance measures should be reviewed and revised as needed to keep the organization competitive and productive. Employees must be involved in the process so that they are aware of what they need to accomplish so that the organization achieves its goals. Reporting requirements should be put into place to provide consistent and uniform measurements. A performance measurement system requires future planning so that the organization can evaluate its strategies and take advantage of new opportunities. The measurements should be optimized so that all departments benefit. And, management must be committed to using the performance measurement results in order for the process to benefit the organization.

Use of Variance Analysis When Measuring Performance

A variance is the difference between a budgeted, planned, or standard amount and the actual costs or sales. Variance analysis attempts to find a cause for the differences between standard or budgeted costs and actual costs. Variance analysis also looks at the effect that a variance has on an organization. When actual costs are less than standard or budgeted costs, the variance is favorable. When actual costs are more than standard or budgeted costs, the variance is unfavorable. When a variance is unfavorable, the reason needs to be determined so that corrective action can be taken. In addition, by uncovering the causes of unfavorable variances, management is better able to serve the organization. Management gains an understanding of the problems an organization faces which helps in setting goals, planning future business opportunities, controlling costs, evaluating performance, and avoiding future problems.

Revenue Center, Cost Center, Profit Center, and Investment Center

A revenue center is a department or division within an organization that generates income. Revenue centers are usually considered profit centers because it is assumed that the revenue center will earn more income than the costs it incurs. A cost center is a department or division within an organization that is only responsible for costs. A cost center has no control over income and does not generate any income. Examples of cost centers are data entry, records retention, human resources, assembly, and production departments. A profit center is a department or division within an organization that creates an income that is separate from other departments within the organization. The profit center may be limited to a product line, a geographical area, a single retail outlet, or a manufacturing unit. An investment center is a division or department within an organization that has control over costs, revenues, and investments. The investment center of an organization is usually the corporate office of an organization or the upper management of a division within the organization.

Direct Materials Variances

Direct materials variances occur when there is a difference between the actual cost of materials and the standard cost of materials. When there is a difference between actual cost and standard cost, this is most likely due to either more or less raw material being used than expected or the price of the raw materials was different than the expected cost. The direct material total variance is the difference between the actual cost of the total number of units produced and the budgeted cost. There are two components of the direct material total variance – the direct material price variance and the direct material quantity variance. The direct material price variance is calculated as the actual cost less the standard cost, multiplied by the actual quantity used. The direct material quantity variance is the actual quantity of material used less the standard quantity of materials that was expected to be used, multiplied by the standard cost per unit of material.

Budget Variances

Budget variances are the differences between budget amounts and actual amounts. It is calculated by taking the actual costs, subtracting the standard (or budgeted) costs, and multiplying the result by the standard units of activity. Budget variances can be analyzed using two different methods – the two-way analysis and the three way analysis. Two-way analysis includes the direct material price variance, the direct material quantity variance, the direct labor price variance, the direct labor quantity variance, the factory overhead spending variance, and the factory overhead efficiency variance. Three-way analysis is a measure of the spending, efficiency, and volume variances for factory overhead. Three-way analysis is used when factory overhead is separated into fixed and variable costs.

Fixed Overhead Variances

The fixed overhead variance is a measure of the difference between the actual fixed overhead and the applied fixed overhead. There are two fixed overhead variances – the fixed overhead spending variance and the fixed overhead volume variance. The fixed overhead spending variance is the difference between the actual fixed overhead incurred and the budgeted fixed overhead. It is calculated by subtracting budgeted fixed overhead from actual fixed overhead. When the fixed overhead spending variance is unfavorable, it may be due to changes in rent, insurance, or taxes. The fixed overhead volume variance is a measure of how well an organization uses its manufacturing facilities. It is measured using direct labor hours, machine hours, or some other quantifiable measure. It is calculated by subtracting the applied fixed overhead from the budged fixed overhead. When the fixed overhead volume variance is unfavorable (that is, when actual levels are greater than budged levels), it may be due to equipment malfunctions, inefficient manufacturing schedules, or the inability to meet productivity goals.

Direct Labor Cost Variances

The direct labor cost variances occur when there is a difference between the standard costs of actual production and the actual costs of production. There are two components of the direct labor cost variance – the direct labor price variance and the direct labor quantity variance. The direct labor price variance is the actual cost per labor hour less the standard cost per hour, multiplied by the actual number of labor hours. The direct labor quantity variance is the estimated amount of labor hours less the actual labor hours used, multiplied by the standard labor rate. The goal is to have the actual hours used be less than the estimated labor hours. This situation shows that labor time is being used efficiently. For labor to be efficient, automation and efficient production methods must be in place.

Sales Variances

Sales variances are used to calculate the difference between actual sales and budgeted sales. There are two different sales variances – the sales price variance and the sales volume variance. The sales volume variance is broken down into two variances – the sales mix variance and the sales quantity variance. A sales variance can occur when an organization increases or decreases the sales price of a product and does not make changes in the budget to reflect this price change. Sales variances can also occur when there are changes in the number of units sold.

Variable Overhead Variances

There are two variable overhead variances -- the variable overhead spending variance and the variable overhead efficiency variance. The variable overhead spending variance is a measure of the difference between actual and budgeted variable overhead costs. This difference may be the result of fluctuations in the price of indirect materials or indirect labor. It may also be the result of a lack of cost control of overhead costs. The variable overhead spending variance is computed by first taking the actual overhead costs and then subtracting the standard rate multiplied by the actual labor hours used. The variable overhead efficiency variance is a measure of the difference between actual and budgeted variable overhead costs. When the variance is unfavorable, this difference is the result of inefficient use of indirect materials and indirect labor. The variable overhead efficiency variance is calculated by subtracting the standard labor hours budgeted for actual production from the actual labor hours, and multiplying this result by the standard variable overhead rate. To obtain a favorable variable overhead efficiency variance measurement, labor should be used efficiently by incorporating automation techniques, efficient production methods should be incorporated into the manufacturing process, and management performance should be optimum.

Sales Volume Variance

The sales volume variance is a calculation that measures the difference between actual sales and expected sales. The sales volume variance determines how well an organization has performed in terms of sales volume. It is measured by subtracting the budgeted number of sales units from the actual number of units sold and then multiplying this result by the budgeted sales price per unit. If the result is a positive number, then the variance is favorable meaning that actual sales were greater than expected sales. If the result is a negative number, then the variance is unfavorable meaning that actual sales were lower than expected. The sales volume variance can be further sub-divided into the sales mix variance and the sales quantity variance.

Sales Price Variance

The sales price variance is a calculation that measures the difference between the actual sales per unit and the budgeted sales per unit. It is measured by subtracting the budgeted sales price per unit from the actual sales price per unit and the multiplying the result by the actual number of units sold. If the result is a positive number, then the variance is favorable meaning that the actual sales were greater than the expected sales. If the result is a negative number, then the variance is unfavorable meaning that actual sales did not meet expectations.

Yield Variances Calculation

Yield variances measure the effect that changes in the total inputs of a production factor has on the weighted average unit price of the production factor. The total inputs can be either direct labor or direct materials. When making this calculation, the input mix is held constant. The input mix consists of the proportion of materials and labor used. Simply stated, the yield variance measures the difference between actual yield and standard yield. It is also an indication of productivity. When a yield variance is unfavorable, it may be due to the use of inferior materials, inefficient labor, malfunctioning equipment, high priced material, or high priced labor. There are two yield variances – the material yield variance and the labor yield variance. The material yield variance is calculated by taking the actual units used at the standard mix, subtracting the actual output units used at the standard mix, and multiplying the result by the standard unit price. The labor yield variance is calculated by taking the actual hours used at the standard mix, subtracting the actual output hours used at the standard mix, and multiplying the result by the standard hourly rate.

Sales Mix Variance

The sales mix variance is a calculation that measures the effect that a product mix has on profits. The product mix is the collection of all of the products or product lines sold by an organization. An organization can have a large product mix where it sells many differing products to large consumer groups. Or, it may have a small product mix where it sells only a few products to a particular consumer group. There is a sales mix variance when different products have different contribution margins. The sales mix variance is computed by subtracting the actual sales at the actual mix from the actual sales and the budgeted mix and multiplying the result by the budgeted contribution margin per unit. The sales mix variance is an indication of how well a department, division, or organization has performed in selling its more profitable products.

Production Mix Variances

A production mix variance is the difference between the standard or budgeted production mix and the actual production mix. It is an indication of how well mixing operations are performed. These mixing operations may be a result of using different amounts of materials or labor to produce a product. The production mix variances show the difference in quantities produced from this change in the production mix. There are two different production mix variances – the material mix variance and the labor mix variance. The material mix variance shows how materials costs are impacted when there is a change in the mix. The material mix variance is calculated by taking the actual units used at the standard mix, subtracting the actual units used at the actual mix, and multiplying the result by the standard unit price. The labor mix variance shows how labor costs change when there is a change in the labor mix. The labor mix variance is calculated by taking the actual hours used at the standard mix, subtracting the actual hours used at the actual mix, and multiplying the result by the standard hourly rate. Production mix variances can be caused by the substitution of inputs, scheduling changes, availability of labor, and availability of materials.

Management by Exception

Management by exception is a management practice where management spends the majority of its time analyzing those activities where actual results are significantly different from planned results. The reasoning behind management by exception is that management should concentrate its efforts on ways to obtain an organization's goals and how to achieve desired performance and productivity. To accomplish this, management only focuses on those areas where deviations from expected performance and budgeted financial figures are lower than the actual results. The causes of these deviations are investigated using decision support systems, expert systems, and performance reporting. These systems can help identify the amount of the variance and the reason for the variance. Once the variance is determined, possible courses of action can be determined and the most successful course of action can be implemented.

Purpose of Responsibility Accounting

Responsibility accounting encompasses collecting, summarizing, and reporting financial information for responsibility centers. These responsibility centers are the basis of decision making and include cost centers, profit centers, revenue centers, and investment centers. Responsibility accounting is a key ingredient in the decision making process because costs, revenues, and profits are tracked for each responsibility center. It holds the managers of these responsibility centers accountable for the decisions they make concerning costs, revenues, and profits. It also makes these managers responsible for taking action if there are variances between actual results and expected results. In responsibility accounting, management's performance is evaluated based on how well the costs, revenues, and profits meet expected results. Responsibility accounting systems are designed so that revenue and cost information is collected and reported by area of responsibility.

Standard Cost System

A standard cost is a predetermined cost that an organization wishes to attain. The assumption is that operating conditions are efficient and that all other variables are perfect. In a standard cost system, all costs are evaluated based on the variance between the actual cost and the standard cost. Standard cost systems are used to evaluate performance of a department, division, or other reporting center in an organization. Standard cost systems are used to control costs, evaluate performance, prepare budgets, value inventory, and motivate employees. By evaluating the difference between standard and actual costs, the causes of the variation can be determined and corrected. This problem determination and analysis activity helps formulate future goals, set attainable cost levels, and determine performance levels.

Purpose of Strategic Business Units

A strategic business unit is a division, a product line, or a product that can be considered a separate entity within an organization. The strategic business unit has its own objectives and mission. Large organizations are usually divided into strategic business units. By dividing up the business in this manner, an organization is better able to serve defined market segments where each market segment requires individual strategic planning for the products and customers served. Each strategic business unit is managed as though it were a separate entity. Each strategic business unit is responsible for meeting its individual performance goals, for adhering to its individual business strategies, setting its individual objectives, for competing in its individual market, and for serving its individual customers.

Contribution Margin

The contribution margin is a cost accounting method used by organizations to determine the profitability of its products. It is normally calculated by taking the total product revenues and subtracting the total variable costs for the product. This is also referred to as the gross operating margin for a product. The contribution margin is the amount of money that is left over that can be used to pay fixed costs and to produce profits. It is usually expressed as the percentage of each sale that remains after the variable costs are subtracted. The purpose of the contribution margin is to see if a product's variable costs are manageable or if the product's price is realistic. If a product's variable costs are not manageable, management may decide to look at ways to reduce the variable costs. Or, management may decide to discontinue the product and look for other another product that can be produced at a lower cost. Contribution margins are also used to decide how to structure sales commissions and bonuses.

Contribution margins are an important part of cost-volume-profit analysis and break-even analysis. Contribution margins determine how much of each unit sold is used to cover fixed costs. There are several contribution margin formulas that can be used. The break-even point in units is the fixed costs divided by the unit contribution margin. The break-even point in dollars is the fixed costs divided by the contribution margin ratio. The target income volume in units is the fixed costs plus the target income divided by the contribution margin. The target income volume in dollars is the fixed costs plus the target income divided by the contribution margin ratio. Contribution margins can tell an organization when it would be profitable to sell a product at a lower price when it has idle capacity. Idle capacity can be used to increase profits or help pay fixed costs when equipment and labor is not being used to its fullest. Contribution margin also tells an organization how well a department or management is performing.

Contribution Margin Income Statements

Contribution margin income statements organize costs incurred by an organization, division, or product line by behavior. The behavior is divided into fixed and variable costs. The purpose of the contribution margin income statement is to make it easy to determine the contribution margin for a product. The contribution margin income statement shows total sales for the product. It then subtracts the variable cost of sales and the variable selling and administrative expenses from sales to come up with the contribution margin. Next, fixed overhead and fixed selling and administrative expenses are subtracted from the contribution margin to determine the net income.

Stand-Alone Cost Allocation and Incremental Cost Allocation

Stand-alone cost allocation is a cost allocation method that divides costs between responsibility centers, departments, products, or another unit based on the use of the cost. The ratio used is calculated by dividing the stand-alone cost of the benefit to the unit divided by the total stand-alone costs. Incremental cost allocation is a variation of the stand-alone cost allocation method. The incremental cost allocation method prioritizes each unit and then allocates the common costs to the priority unit up to the amount of that unit's stand-alone costs. The common costs that remain are allocated to the other units.

Cost Allocation

Cost allocation is a method where costs are associated with cost objectives. Cost allocation is also called cost apportionment, cost assignment, cost distribution, and cost reapportionment. Cost allocation involves the selection of the object to be tracked (such as a product, a process, a job, or a department), accumulating the costs that relate to the object (such as production expenses, sales expenses, or administrative expenses), and selecting a method that identifies the cost with the object (such as labor hours, machine hours, or production units). Costs are usually allocated to a cost object based on cause-and-effect, benefits received, fairness, and ability to pay the cost. When a cost is for a long-term asset that spans two or more time periods, the allocation of costs is based on depreciation, depletion, or amortization. Costs that occur within a single time period (usually one year or less) are allocated to a responsibility center, a product, or a service. Costs allocated to a responsibility center are used to motivate management to be goal oriented.

Negotiated Transfer Pricing Method

Negotiated transfer pricing occurs when two divisions within an organization discuss the price at which they will buy and sell a product. When used within a multi-division organization, negotiated transfer pricing helps each division retain autonomy. Problems may occur when divisions cannot agree on a transfer price. When this type of situation arises, it may be necessary for the two divisions to call in a mediator or arbitrator to help formulate an agreed upon price. In order to circumvent this type of situation where a transfer price cannot be agreed upon, some organizations establish arbitrary procedures to prevent disputes from arising.

Transfer Pricing

Transfer pricing is a method used to allocate costs between profit centers. The function of transfer pricing is to set prices for services, evaluate financial performance, and determine the contribution a profit center makes to net income. Transfer pricing uses one of five pricing methods – market-based price, cost-based price, full cost price, variable cost price, or negotiated transfer price. The market price is the actual amount paid for the cost. The cost-based price is the marginal cost of funds. The negotiated priced is set by agreement between the buyer and the seller. Transfer pricing is used when a product or service is sold between divisions or departments within an organization.

Cost-Based Pricing Method

Cost-based pricing is when the cost base is either the variable cost or the full cost of the product being sold. This method is easy to use and understand. On the negative side, there is no incentive to control costs with the cost-based pricing method. With this method, increased costs because of cost control and manufacturing inefficiencies are passed on to the buyer. If there are cost inefficiencies on the seller's side of the transaction, it would more advantageous for the buyer to use the standard cost as the basis of the transfer price. Also, in cost-based pricing, it is hard to use return on investment and residual income calculations to evaluate the profitability of the transfer price. This is because the cost-based pricing method classifies each division as a cost center and not as a profit center or an investment center.

Market-Based Pricing Method

Market-based pricing uses a sales price that gives the organization the most profit potential. Before market-based pricing can be used, there must be a competitive market for the product and an established market price. Also, the divisions must be separate entities within the organization and have independent product mixes and management. When market-based pricing is used, it gives each division the freedom to buy and sell products within the organization and outside the organization. This method allows each division to retain independence from other divisions. In addition, by being able to act independently, each division conducts business in a manner that is most profitable for the entire organization.

Variable Pricing Method

Variable cost pricing is a transfer pricing method where different prices are charged to different customers or are charged at different time periods. Variable cost pricing may be used to give discounts to customers who purchase significantly high quantities of a product. Also, variable cost pricing may occur because seller and buyer have negotiated on the sales price of the product. Variable cost pricing may also be used to charge different prices at different times of the year. This may be done to increase sales during a normally low sales period. Variable cost pricing may provide the best utilization of an organization's resources. This is because fixed costs do not change and any use of idle resources that do not increase fixed costs will increase profitability.

Full Cost Pricing Method

Full cost pricing is a transfer pricing method that uses the total manufacturing cost per unit as the cost base. Added to the base is a markup. This markup covers fixed costs such as selling and administrative costs. The markup is computed by taking the total fixed costs and dividing by the estimated number of units that will be sold. This markup is added to the cost base which is the variable cost per unit. The variable costs include direct material costs, direct labor costs, and factory overhead costs. This gives the true unit cost. To establish a sales price, a return on sales is added to the true unit cost. The full cost pricing method establishes a sales price that approximates the market price. The benefit of the full cost pricing method is that it is easy to calculate a sales price and does not require a large amount of information to determine the base price. The disadvantage of full cost pricing is that it does not promote efficient business operations because the division is guaranteed of covering costs.

Standards Used for Performance Evaluation and Measurement

Standards are used in performance evaluation by measuring efficiency and costs. Every organization sets standards for the expected output for each employee or process, the time required to accomplish a task or complete a process, and the allowable and acceptable levels for mistakes, waste, and spoilage. Standards keep tasks within an allowable time frame and determine the scope of the task. Standards keep tasks from going beyond what is practical and necessary. When standards are achievable, employees can realistically meet or exceed goals. If an employee cannot achieve the standards, improvement on the part of the employee is needed. When standards are ideal, goals may not be able to be met. Ideal standards represent a perfect operating environment. In most cases, it is impossible to achieve ideal standards. When an ideal standard is not met, there is usually nothing an employee can do to improve performance.

Taxes on Transfer Pricing Transactions

For transfer pricing to be profitable for multinational corporations, the organization must select prices so that it earns the majority of its profit in the country of business that has the lowest tax rate. This shifts the tax burden around, so that overall, the organization is paying lower taxes thereby increasing profits. When using transfer pricing in this method, the organization must be aware of government regulations that may limit how transfer prices can be set. When these regulations are not adhered to, it may mean that the organization will have to pay taxes and penalties in excess of any gains it may have received from the transfer pricing transactions. On the other hand, the transfer pricing regulations can provide protection from double taxation for a multinational corporation. This advantage can usually be found when the transfer pricing transaction is between countries that have bilateral tax treaties.

Return on Investment (ROI)

Return on investment is a measure of the amount of money that is gained on an investment. It is calculated by taking the gain realized from an investment, subtracting the cost of the investment, and dividing the result by the cost of the investment. Return on investment is used to measure the efficiency of an investment or to determine how well an investment performs compared to other investments. The disadvantage of return on investment is that the calculation can be manipulated to fit within a desired situation. This can be done by modifying what is considered a return and what is considered a cost. Costs used to determine return on investment can vary. For example, one calculation may only consider the realized expenses incurred on behalf of the investment (such as commissions). Another calculation may also add the economic costs of the investment (such as lost income from not investing in another asset).

Return on Investment Use

Return on investment can be used to measure investment options and business operations. When measuring how well an organization is using its invested equity (shareholder investment), the return on investment calculation takes the net income and divides that amount by invested capital. This measurement provides an indication of an organization's profitability. This measure of profitability can then be compared with the organization's competition or with an industry average to determine how well an organization is performing. Return on investment can be used to determine how well a division or product line is performing. This measurement can determine how well a division or product uses its invested capital to earn a profit. It can also be used to determine if a division or product requires further investment. Return on investment is also used to determine whether an investment should be undertaken. This calculation is performed by dividing the increase in profit that will be realized with the investment by the amount of capital needed to make the investment. If this calculation yields a number that is higher than the interest that will be paid on the debt needed to acquire the investment, it may be a reasonable investment.

Book to Market Ratio

The book to market ratio is a method of valuation that compares an organization's book value to its market value. Book value is the value of an organization's stock based on historical or accounting value. Market value is the price at which the stock is selling on an exchange market. The book to market ratio is computed by dividing the book value by the market value. The book to market ratio is used to determine whether an organization's stock is undervalued or overvalued. A stock is undervalued when the book to market ratio is greater than 1.

Earnings Quality

Earnings quality is the amount of earnings that are due to an increase in sales or a decrease in costs. Increases in earnings due to an increase in asset valuation are not a part of earnings quality. These earnings are due to inflation. When balance sheet items are inflated, an organization's earnings quality tends to fall. When an organization has increased sales and can lower costs, its earnings quality will rise.

Basic Earnings Per Share

Basic earnings per share is one of two ways in which an organization reports its earnings per share. Basic earnings per share does not account for stock options, warrants, and convertible securities. Basic earnings per share is computed by dividing the net income available to common shareholders by the number of share outstanding. Net income available to common shareholders is computed by subtracting declared preferred dividends from net income.

Price-Earnings Ratio

The price-earnings ratio is a method of valuing the market share price of an organization's stock compared to its earnings per share. It is calculated by dividing market value per share by earnings per share. The price-earnings ratio shows how much an investor pays for a share of stock for each dollar of earnings. A high price-earnings ratio means that investors are paying more for a stock than it earns. It also means that investors expect to see higher earnings in the future to make up for this difference. The higher the price-earnings ratio, the riskier the stock is as an investment.

EARNING POWER

Earning power is the ability of an organization to earn a profit after it has paid all of its obligations. Earning power is an indication of business risk. The earning power of an organization is used by banks and other institutions when considering loan applications. Earning power is also used to determine whether an organization is solvent.

DILUTED EARNINGS PER SHARE

Diluted earnings per share are a method of reporting earnings per share that shows how stock option grants and convertible bonds effect earnings per share. It is used to show a worst case scenario. It takes into account how stock that is held but has not been paid for decreases earnings per share.

RATIO ANALYSIS

Ratio analysis is a method used to perform comparisons, formulate forecasts, and help make decisions when looking at financial statement information. Ratios can be used to look at an organization's performance, its productivity, its financial health, its growth, and its potential for future growth and solvency.

EARNINGS YIELD

Earnings yield is the amount of earnings that is derived from each dollar of stock. It is computed by dividing the earnings per share by the market price for each share of stock. Earnings yield is used to compare the value of a stock against bond yields. It is also used to determine the cost to an organization of raising capital through a stock issue.

ECONOMIC PROFIT

Economic profit differs from accounting profit in that economic profit takes opportunity costs into account. Opportunity costs are the result of opportunities or alternatives that were not pursued in favor of the selected course of action. The opportunity cost is the income that could have been realized from the foregone course of action. Economic profit is calculated at accounting profit less opportunity costs.

ACCOUNTING PROFIT

Accounting profit is the profit that an organization earns when the financial records of the organization are prepared in accordance with generally accepted accounting principles. Accounting profit is income less expenses. Expenses include all of those costs of doing business including cost of goods sold, depreciation, interest payable, and taxes. Simply put, to calculate accounting profits, subtract the cost of producing products or services from total revenues.

MARKET VALUE

Market value is the price at which shares of stock sell in a financial market. Market value is based on what investors are willing to pay for an organization's stock. This price is determined by a number of factors such as availability of the stock, the financial ratios, and speculation about the organization's future.

BOOK VALUE

Book value is the amount of money that a common shareholder would receive if an organization were liquidated. This would be the funds left over after all assets were sold and all debts paid. Book value is calculated by first subtracting preferred equity from total shareholder equity and then dividing the sum by the total number of shares outstanding.

Residual Income (RI)

Residual income is a measure of the amount of operating income that an investment earns that is above a minimum level of return on assets. Residual income is calculated by multiplying the minimum rate of return expected on an investment by operating assets and subtracting this figure from net operating income. Residual income is a method of measuring performance. It can be used to compare the performance of separate organizations or to compare the performance of divisions within an organization. There are many advantages to using residual income as a performance measurement. The opportunity costs of using an asset are taken into consideration when computing residual income. The minimum rate of return on the investment is not a concrete figure and can be adjusted based on the risk level of the investment. Also, residual income places the emphasis on maximizing a total dollar return instead of emphasizing a percentage return.

Dupont Model Method of Calculating Return on Assets

The Dupont Method was created by the Dupont Corporation in the 1920s. It was used as a measure of performance by valuing assets at gross book value instead of valuing assets at net book value. By using gross book value, a higher return on investment is achieved. The reasoning behind this is that accounting methods include depreciation in the return on investment calculation which produces an artificially low return on investment in the first few years that an investment is placed in service. The Dupont Method uses sales figures to measure profitability. The Dupont Model is calculated by multiplying operating margin by turnover. Operating margin is earnings before interest and taxes divided by sales. Turnover is sales divided by average total assets.

Economic Value Added (EVA)

Economic value added is a method used to measure the financial performance of an organization by looking at the economic profit of the organization. Economic value added uses residual wealth as the basis of financial performance. Residual wealth is calculated by deducting the cost of capital from operating profit. Economic value added measures economic profit after deducting the opportunity cost of equity capital. Economic value added is calculated by multiplying capital by the cost of capital and subtracting the result from the net operating profit after taxes. Economic value added is different from residual income calculations. Residual income uses the market or book value of assets to value the capital invested. Economic value added uses the market value of the total investment and interest bearing debt.

Return on Investment (ROI) and Residual Income (RI)

Residual income measures an absolute amount of income. Return on investment measures a rate of return. Residual income is used to evaluate performance based on an excess of income over the expected income. The objective of residual income is to attain the highest level of residual income. The objective of return on investment is to attain the highest return on investment percentage. Residual income is preferred over return on investment as a performance measurement because it promotes investment opportunities that have a higher rate of return than the cost of invested capital. When return on investment is used as a performance measurement, investment opportunities that lower the rate of return will not be undertaken, even if the investment would be beneficial to the organization.

Cash Flow Return on Investment

Cash flow return on investment is an equity valuation method that uses cash flow as the base and not earnings as the base. Cash flow return on investment is used by financial markets to determine stock prices. It is calculated by dividing cash flow by market capitalization. Cash flow return on investment can also be thought of as the internal rate of return for an organization. Cash flow return on investment is used in conjunction with a hurdle rate to determine if an investment or a product is performing to expected standards. A hurdle rate is the total cost of capital. This cost of capital is the cost of debt financing and the expected return on equity investments.

Market Value Added

Market value added is the difference between the market value of an organization and the capital invested by shareholders and bondholders. It is calculated by adding all of the capital claims held and the market value of debt and equity. When the result of the market value added calculation is positive, this means that the organization has created wealth for its shareholders. When the result of the market value added calculation is negative, the organization has taken action and made investments that are lower than the value contributed to the organization by shareholders and bondholders. For an organization to be seen positively by investors, the market value added should be more than the amount that investors would be able to realize from investing in a diversified market portfolio.

Key Performance Indicators

A Key Perforance Indicator (KPI) helps an organization define and measure progress toward it's goals. A KPI is a quantifiable measurement that can be used to monitor progress on a specific goal. For example, a company has the goal to "be the most profitable company the industry". It will have KPI's that measure profit and other fiscal measures. These might include "Pre-tax profit" and "Shareholder Equity", but would not iclude measures like "Percent of profit donated" or "Stock price". The main thing to remember is that KPI's must always be measurable, so that progress can be tracked.

Evaluating an Organization Using Learning and Growth, Business Processes, and Customers

Learning and growth, business processes, and customers are an indication of an organization's future growth because these factors do not take historical results into effect. When these factors are analyzed, balance within the organization and its future success can be achieved. The factors of finances, customers, business processes, and innovation are considered to be a balanced set of dimensions upon which performance can be assessed. These factors combine the characteristics of quantitative measures and qualitative measures which can be measured against each other. For example, a quantitative measure, such as the number of units output, can be measured against a qualitative measure, such as customer satisfaction. These factors can also be used to measure past performance to get an indication of future performance. For example, growth in sales and new products can be used to predict the number of new products that will be developed in the future.

Balanced Scorecard

A balanced scorecard is a method used in the strategic management process where internal functions are identified so that improvement procedures can be implemented. These internal functions and the resulting external outcomes are measured so that feedback can be provided on strategies and objectives that will result in improved operations. The purpose of the balanced scorecard approach is to help management make long-term decisions that will result in added value to the organization's shareholders. The areas that the balanced scorecard analyzes include learning and growth, business processes, customers, and finance. Learning and growth measurements determine an organization's ability to adapt to new situations, use innovative techniques, and create growth. Business processes are analyzed to determine the organization's success in improving its internal operations. The customer base of the organization is analyzed to ensure that the organization is meeting customers' expectations. The financial situation of the organization is analyzed so that shareholders and creditors evaluate the organization favorably.

Implementing the Balanced Scorecard Concept

There are four processes involved in implementing the balanced scorecard concept. The first process is to determine the vision of the organization and turn that vision into operational goals. This requires that the organization focus on the future and decide which actions will benefit the organization in the long-term. The second process is to communicate the vision with management and staff so that everyone involved in the organization understands their role in meeting the organization's goals. This process also involves communicating responsibilities and ensuring that everyone understands how their performance is related to meeting these goals. The third process is business planning. This is the strategic management process that gives management the tools needed to ensure the organization's success. The fourth process is feedback and learning. This process is important because it provides the tools needed to measure how well goals are being met. If goals are not being met, then changes can be made in the functioning or the organization or adjustments can be made to the strategy.

Balanced Scorecard Approach to Performance Evaluation

The balanced scorecard approach is a non-financial measure of performance evaluation. The goal of the balanced scorecard approach is continuous quality improvement. The balanced scorecard approach uses several performance measurements. Each performance measurement indicates how well the objectives of the organization are being met. These performance measurements are linked to financial outcomes, customer outcomes, and business process outcomes. Examples of financial outcomes include the standard cost of raw materials, standard labor hours, and forecasted units of production. Examples of customer outcomes include customer satisfaction, product returns, number of customer orders, growth in new customers, and market share. Examples of business process outcomes include number of defects, production time, backlogs, lost production days, employee turnover, and level of employee work experience.

Learning and Growth Measures Included in the Balanced Scorecard Concept

The learning and growth measures include employee training, employee self-improvement, and organizational self-improvement. People are the major knowledge resource in an organization. It is imperative that the individual and the organization ensure that existing knowledge is continually being updated and new knowledge added to the information base. The individual and the organization must be in a constant learning mode. This constant learning ensures that the organization is able to keep up with technological advances and to stay competitive in its industry. The learning process includes training new employees, training employees in new processes, mentoring employees to help them perform to their best ability, and tutoring employees so that they can grow within their job function. Learning and growth also encompasses a communication aspect where employees are able to get help when they encounter a problem and have access to the proper tools to help them learn and deal with problems.

Use of Balanced Scorecard

The balanced scorecard concept is a tool used in performance management. It is used to help management understand and implement an organization's strategy. Management uses the balanced scorecard concept to focus on strategic issues and to manage the performance of an organization's strategy. The balanced scorecard concept does not play any role in the strategic planning process. Organizations can use the balanced scorecard concept in many ways. It can be used to formulate budgets and to keep budgets updated. It can be used to identify strategic initiatives and ensure that those initiatives are kept within the organization's goals. It is also used to perform performance reviews. The information gained in performance reviews is then used to determine whether goals are being met and to decide if strategy measures needed to be revised.

Balanced Scorecard Concept Customer Measures

The customer measures focus on the customers' needs and the customers' satisfaction with the products and services provided by the organization. The customers' needs and satisfaction are important indicators because customers can go elsewhere if they are not happy with an organization's product or performance. Even if an organization's financial measurements look good, poor customer satisfaction may lead to a decline in financial performance. When determining customer satisfaction results, the organization should look at the types of customers they are servicing, the processes that provide the product or service to the customer, the organization's market share for a product, the organization's ability to retain customers, the organization's ability to respond to customer needs, and the organization's ability to deliver product.

Balanced Scorecard Concept Business Process Measures

The business process measures are those internal business processes that give an organization an indication of how well the business is operating. It also determines how well an organization performs at developing products that meet customer requirements and how well its services meet customer satisfaction levels. The business processes measured are mission-oriented processes and support processes. Mission-oriented processes are those processes that are essential to meeting organizational goals. Mission-oriented processes may include the ability to keep up with technology and creating a more efficient manufacturing environment. Support processes are those processes that meet the needs of the customer. These support processes may include the introduction of new products and ability to meet customer demands for a product.

Goal Congruence

Goal congruence occurs when the actions of management and employees are in agreement with the goals of the organization. When the goals of employees and management are aligned with the goals of the organization, the organization will achieve its goals productively and efficiently. To attain goal congruence, management must have the motivation to put forth the managerial effort that is necessary to attain a goal. Management must also have the commitment to accomplish the goal. The managerial effort includes both psychological and physical commitment to accomplish a goal. The major factors that lead to goal congruence include cooperation by management and employees with the organization, coordination of goals at all levels of the organization, and knowledge of the goals and the expected outcome.

Cost Management

Cost Management

Cost management is the management and control of organizational planning activities. These activities include the formulation of strategies, determination of product costs, improvement of business processes, reduction of waste and costs, identification of cost drivers, and planning of business operations. Cost management uses cost accounting as the basis for managing and controlling the costs of doing business.

Purpose of Cost Management

The purpose of cost management is the continual control of costs. Controlling costs is important in business management because the costs of doing business affect revenue and profits. The goal of cost management is to increase customer satisfaction, lower production and administration costs, and thereby increase profits and earnings. The decisions made in the cost control process come from accounting systems and financial information provided by those accounting systems.

Controllability

Controllability is the ability of a manager to influence those individuals that perform tasks, incur costs, and generate revenues. The controllability efforts of managers include monitoring costs, determining where costs can be reduced, and taking steps to reduce costs. In order to control costs, managers must decide how employees should perform jobs and tasks and then develop procedures that will ensure the jobs and tasks are completed in a timely and efficient manner. The annual budget is the foundation of the cost control process. The actual costs for the budget period are compared to the annual budget and the evaluation process helps set new plans that help reduce costs and increase revenues. The annual budget in conjunction with accounting controls establishes organization objectives, determines centers of responsibility, and designs procedures for reporting and evaluation.

Common Costs

Common costs are also called indirect costs. A common cost is a cost or expense that is distributed among several departments, products, tasks, or jobs. Examples of common costs are electricity for an entire manufacturing facility, real estate taxes, advertising that benefits more than one product or sales region, and insurance premiums. It is often difficult to assign common costs equitably between the departments, products, tasks, or jobs that share the cost. Many times, common costs are distributed on an arbitrary basis. When common costs are allocated on a cause and effect basis, there is a relationship between the cost and the actions of the cost object. This method enables managers and employees to see the allocation of the cost as fair and equitable. Costs may also be allocated based on the benefit received. Only those departments or products that see an increase in revenue from the cost incurred are allocated a portion of the cost based on the increase received.

Approaches to Common Cost Allocation

There are two approaches to common cost allocation – the stand-alone method and the incremental method. The stand-alone method of common cost allocation uses the benefit received as the basis of the cost allocation. A portion of the common costs is allocated to each department, product, task, or job by applying a proportionate share of the total cost based on each unit's use of the cost. The incremental method of common cost allocation allocates the common costs up to the amount of the unit's stand-alone costs. The primary user of the cost is allocated costs first and the rest of the common costs are allocated to the rest of the units.

Cost of Goods Sold Expenses

The cost of goods sold is the sum of those costs that are incurred in the production of products. It includes direct material expenses, direct labor expenses, and overhead expenses. These expenses can be either fixed or variable.

Prime Cost

A prime cost is the sum of direct material and direct labor costs. Overhead is not included in the prime cost. Direct material costs are the costs of materials that are a part of a finished product. Direct labor costs are the costs of the labor that are directly involved in producing a finished product.

Overhead Cost

Overhead cost is the sum of all manufacturing costs except direct materials and direct labor. An overhead cost is an expense that is ongoing and necessary to operate a business, a piece of equipment, or a facility. These costs are necessary to ensure continued operation of the organization but do not necessarily contribute to the net profits or losses of the organization. Business overhead costs are those resources that maintain an organization's existence. Examples of business overhead costs are rent, utilities, business permits, business registration fees, administrative personnel costs, and liability insurance. Equipment operating costs are those expenses that are necessary to operate a piece of equipment but do not include the capital cost of building or purchasing the equipment. Equipment overhead costs include labor costs, materials, fuel costs, maintenance, and depreciation. Overhead costs may be fixed costs or variable costs.

Conversion Cost

A conversion cost occurs when an organization changes from one type of business or manufacturing process to another. Examples include converting from a labor intensive assembly method to a robotic system of assembly. Another example is the conversion from blueprint drafting methods to computer aided design. The costs included in the conversion are the cost of the new equipment, and the costs incurred in training personnel in the use of the new equipment.

Sunk Cost

A sunk cost is an expense that has been paid and cannot be refunded. These are costs that were incurred in the past and present decisions have no effect on the ability to recover the cost. A sunk cost can also be thought of as a cost that has already been paid and does not have any relevant effect on future decisions because the cost is not relevant in the decision making process.

Carrying Cost

Carrying costs are those costs an organization incurs as a result of keeping inventory in stock. Carrying costs include storage costs, taxes, insurance, and the opportunity cost of lost interest on the money invested in the inventory.

Opportunity Cost

An opportunity cost is the cost of choosing one alternative over another. The benefits of the foregone alternative decision less the benefits of the selected alternative are the opportunity cost of the selected alternative. Opportunity costs occur when there is a choice that must be made between two options. The opportunity cost is the risk that the foregone option will provide a greater benefit.

Discretionary Cost

A discretionary cost is an expense that can be easily changed by management's judgment. Examples of discretionary costs are advertising, maintenance and repairs, and research and development. Changes in these costs will have an effect on an organization's future earnings and profitability. Management may decrease discretionary costs when the organization needs funds for other purposes, when cash is critically low, or to decrease a high earnings rate.

Variable Cost

Variable costs are those costs that go up and down depending on the level of manufacturing production. Examples of variable costs are packaging material, raw materials needed to manufacture a product, and assembly labor. As a general rule, variable costs per unit decrease as the level of total production increases. This can be attributed to economies of scale. The amount of the sales price of a product that is above the variable cost is a contribution to the fixed costs of an organization.

Fixed Cost

Fixed costs are those costs of doing business that do not fluctuate depending on the level of production or the time period being considered. These are costs that an organization must incur regardless of the level of business activity. Fixed costs usually include those expenses which are not included in cost of goods sold. Examples of fixed costs are rents, insurance, salaried payroll, and utility bills. Fixed costs do not affect production decisions because fixed costs do not change depending on the level of output.

Direct Cost

A direct cost is an expense that can be directly attributed to one particular project or product. Examples of direct costs are materials and labor that are solely used on one project or product. Direct costs can be either variable or fixed.

Mixed Cost

A mixed cost is a cost that can be divided into both fixed and variable elements. Some utility expenses can be classified as mixed costs. A certain portion of the utility bill is incurred no matter what the usage is and the other portion varies with the amount of usage. The cost of operating a vehicle is also a mixed cost. Certain expenses are fixed, such as insurance and depreciation. Other expenses are variable depending on the usage of the vehicle, such as gasoline and maintenance.

Cost Pool

A cost pool is a group of individual costs. These groups can be defined by department, job, or activity. In a cost pool, expenses are allocated to their appropriate department, job, or activity. Expenses are not kept in a general expense category. For example, the purchase of office supplies are allocated to the cost pools for the different departments that use the supplies, such as reception or sales.

Indirect Cost

An indirect cost is an expense that cannot be easily attached to one particular project or product. An indirect cost is one that is spent for the benefit of several projects or products. Example of indirect costs are advertising, administrative expenses, depreciation, and manufacturing overhead.

Cost Driver

A cost driver is a factor that has a direct relationship to a cost. Cost drivers include items such as labor hours, equipment time used, and miles driven. Cost drivers are used to measure the consumption of an item as it is used by a product, department, or activity. For example, a purchasing department may measure the number of orders placed by customers during a period of time to determine how many labor hours are spent processing each individual customer order. Not all cost drivers can be easily measured. When this is the case, an acceptable substitute will be used.

Cost Object

Cost objects are the intermediate and final distributions of costs pools. Cost pools move from various points within the organization and accumulate costs as they move through the system. The final cost pools are linked to their respective cost objects according to a cause and effect relationship. Using this method, an organization will know what the total amount is for an expense and the cost pool that acquired the expense. The organization will also know what costs have been incurred for each department, process, or job.

Normal Cost

A normal cost is an average of the expenses incurred for a given product over the course of a year. This cost is based on budgeted rates and actual quantity of resources used. Normal costs include actual direct materials, actual direct labor, and applied overhead. These costs are calculated by using a predetermined rate for the actual costs of material, labor, and overhead and multiplying those by the actual units of input. Examples of these inputs are machine hours used and labor hours. A normal cost is not affected by the variation in costs during the year due to changes in production or seasonal fluctuations.

Actual Cost

An actual cost is the expense incurred when an item is purchased or produced. This expense for a purchased item includes the price of the item, any discounts received, delivery fees, and storage costs. The actual cost for a produced item includes direct material costs, direct labor costs, and overhead costs. Actual costs vary during the year with fluctuations in production output and seasonal trends. Reasons for this variance include unscheduled and unexpected equipment repairs, reaching the limit on Social Security payments, and cooling and heating costs for buildings and facilities.

Actual, Budgeted, and Standard Costs

Budgets are a compilation of actual, budgeted, and standard costs. Actual costs are used to show how much of a resource an organization expects to use during the budget period. Budgeted costs are an estimate of what the organization desires to achieve in terms of sales and how much it wants to spend to be able to produce this level of sales. Budgeted costs are based on the actual costs for the previous budget period along with input from management and staff as to changes that could be made to improve efficiency and productivity. Standard costs are derived by determining a cost level that would use resources efficiently and efficiently.

Absorption Costing Method

Absorption costing is a method used to calculate the unit cost of a product by including all costs into the equation. These costs include all overhead costs such as direct material costs, direct labor costs, factory overhead, indirect material costs, indirect labor, administrative expenses, selling expenses, and distribution costs. The overhead costs may be fixed, variable, direct, or indirect. Absorption costing is used to determine profits and capital stock values. Absorption costing is accomplished by recording all costs, classifying these costs, linking costs to output, allocating indirect costs to service and production departments, determining the overhead recovery rate, and finally allocating these costs to the respective products.

Variable Costing Method

Variable costing is a management tool that is used for inventory valuation, cost analysis, breakeven analysis, cost-volume-profit analysis, and decision making. Variable costing is not used in external reporting or income tax reporting. The costs included in the variable costing method include variable manufacturing costs such as direct materials, direct labor, variable overhead, and product cost.

Use of Product Costing

Product costing is used in the evaluation and planning of business strategies by providing accurate product costs. Product costing involves keeping track of all the expenses incurred in the production and sale of a product. It tracks all costs from material purchases to distribution costs. These costs include expenses to acquire and maintain suppliers, transport products to the market, accounts payable costs, inventory costs, warehousing, inventory control, manufacturing costs, product warranties and guarantees, quality control, billing and collection costs, product improvements, and regulatory compliance. For a product costing system to be effective, costs must be accurately distributed among the various products. This system will not work if costs are distributed evenly among products.

Variable Costing and Absorption Costing Affect the Income Statement

When using absorption costing, fixed overhead costs incurred in the current period are deferred to future reporting periods when inventory levels increase. When these inventory items are sold, the fixed overhead costs are reported as a cost of goods sold. Variable costing and absorption costing report inventory figures differently. In variable costing, variable manufacturing costs are included in the inventory figure. In absorption costing, fixed and variable manufacturing costs are included in the inventory figure. When absorption costing is used, the data provided cannot be used for cost-volume-profit analysis because there is no distinction between fixed and variable costs. Variable costing, on the other hand, uses only variable costs which are classified by job or task.

Process Costing

Process costing is an accounting method where costs are distributed to the respective department or production process. Direct materials, direct labor, and overhead are charged to the department or process that uses the cost. To compute the unit cost for the department or process, total costs are divided by units of output. Process costing is most effective in industries that produce only a few products, such as food products, textiles, chemicals, and utilities. To keep track of costs in a process costing system, a schedule of equivalent production, a unit cost analysis schedule, and a cost summary schedule are used. The schedule of equivalent production details the number of units produced over a specified period of time. The unit cost analysis schedule shows the costs charged to the work in process account for the department or process and computes the cost per unit. The cost summary schedule determines the inventory and work in process costs to be distributed to a department or process.

Job Order Costing

Job order costing is an accounting method where costs are distributed to their respective job, contract, or order. This method is used to identify direct costs with a specified unit of production or service. Job order costing is used when an organization performs custom manufacturing jobs where the costs need to be applied to a specific customer's order. The types of activities that are best suited for job order costing include construction, accounting and legal services, printing and publishing, automobile and equipment maintenance, and consulting. In a job order costing system, costs are distributed to the appropriate jobs in a variety of ways. Direct material costs and direct labor costs are easily applied to a specific job. Indirect overhead is applied to each job using a predetermined rate which is usually the budgeted annual overhead divided by the budgeted annual activity unit (such as labor hours or machine hours). If, at the end of the year, there is any unallocated overhead, it is applied to cost of goods sold.

Activity-Based Costing

Activity-based costing is an accounting method that distributes expenses among a range of an organization's products depending on the actions performed within the organization. Each employee's time is allocated between the activities that are performed and each activity is calculated as a percentage of the employee's time to determine the amount of the employee's salary to allocate to that activity. Using this method, the different activities are allocated to the related products. Activity-based costing is used to improve operational efficiency. Activity-based costing shows an organization how much time employees spend on each activity. If too much time is spent on an activity, management may decide if it is necessary to explore possible areas of process efficiency.

Equivalent Units Used in Process Costing

Equivalent units are a way in which a certain number of unfinished units can be considered to be finished units for the purpose of determining the cost of manufacturing. For example, if there are 100 units that are considered unfinished or as work-in-process and those units are determined to be 75% complete, then the equivalent units (or estimated finished units) are 75. To determine the equivalent unit cost, the total cost is divided by the equivalent units. If the total cost to produce a product is $1,000 and there are 75 equivalent units, the equivalent unit cost is $13.33. Equivalent units may also be used to determine direct material costs and conversion costs for unfinished products. When determining direct material costs for equivalent units, only materials that are part of the finished product are considered. When determining conversion costs for equivalent units, the costs of moving from one type of equipment or process to another is considered.

Disadvantages of Activity Based Costing

Activity based costing can be expensive to implement and maintain. The software required to keep track of detailed financial information can cost large sums of money. This type of software can run into many thousands of dollars. The process for keeping track of costs in an activity based costing systems requires that time, effort, and money be expended to collect and analyze the data. This can sometimes be frustrating for those involved in the accounting and decision making functions. In addition, it is not always possible to see the results and benefits of activity based costing immediately. When an organization chooses activity based costing to improve its business processes, it may take several months or more before the organization will see any benefits to the system.

Activity Based Costing and Traditional Costing Systems Differences

In traditional costing systems, indirect costs are added to direct costs for a product or process by using an arbitrarily determined percentage figure. This can result in overhead costs being over or under allocated to departments, processes, or products. In activity based costing, all of the costs that are used in the production of a product are accounted for and distributed based on actual usage. This results in costs that are accurately allocated, allowing organizations to make more informed decisions. Organizations have a better understanding of what products increase profitability and what products create losses because of the greater understanding of what expenses are incurred and how they are used. The more accurate financial figures provided by activity based costing also allow organizations to generate more accurate budgets.

Life-Cycle Costing

Life-cycle costing is an accounting method that keeps track of the income and expenses of a product during its entire life cycle. This life cycle extends from the research and development phases, through the introduction, growth, maturity stages, to the decline stage. The costs included in this method range from research and development, production, marketing, distribution, and customer service. Life-cycle costing is important when making pricing decisions so that costs are covered and profits assured during all phases of the life cycle. These accounting figures can be used to improve efficiency and reduce costs for future product development.

Life-Cycle Costing Use

The purpose of life-cycle costing is to minimize the costs associated with an asset, product, or process. Life-cycle costing uses net present value, internal rate of return, and discounted cash flow methods to minimize future costs. Organizations use life-cycle costing for new product development, product and project evaluations, and management accounting. When analyzing life cycle costs, the cost of a process or product is tracked over the entire life cycle. These costs include, planning, research, production, operations, maintenance, replacement, and salvage. The benefits of life-cycle costing are that all costs associated with a process or product are accounted for, it shows interrelationships between functions or processes, and makes more accurate revenue predictions possible.

Activity Based Costing Used in Service Organizations

Service organizations such as financial institutions, medical facilities, and consulting firms can take advantage of the benefits of activity based costing. Activity based costing is more beneficial for those service organizations that have a broad service line, a diverse product list, and a large customer base. In service organizations, the largest component of the activity based costing system is the labor component. It is beneficial to see how labor hours are spent dealing with products and servicing customers. Because most of the cost in a service organization is direct labor, it is easier to trace this labor cost directly back to the service or product being provided. To measure cost activity for labor, it is necessary to calculate the amount of time an employee works on a process and to tally the number and types of processes completed.

Operation Costing

Operation costing is a cross between job order costing and process costing. It is used by organizations that produce a number of similar products but each individual product is a slight variation of the basic design. In this system, all products go through the same sequence of processes but not all products will go through all of the processes. Operation costing uses total conversion costs to determine a unit conversion cost for each operation in the manufacturing process. Operation costing is used to determine the cost of a product at each stage of its production.

Backflush Costing

Backflush costing is used in just-in-time manufacturing environments. In backflush costing, the costing process is not performed or costs calculated until the products have completed the finished stage. When the production is complete, the costs are tallied and then assigned throughout the system to each product. This eliminates detailed tracing of costs. Backflush costing is best utilized by organizations that hold a low level of inventory. It has many benefits. Expenses are recorded in cost of goods sold. There is no need to keep track of work in progress. Inventory accounting does not take place until the product is completed or sold. Standard costs are used to assign costs to the various products.

Implicit Costs

An implicit cost is an opportunity cost that an organization incurs when it uses its own resources to finance one project over another project. These costs may be from the use of capital, from the use of financial resources, or from the use of management's time. These costs are not actual cash outlays. Implicit costs cannot be deducted in an organization's financial records. The implicit cost is measured by the benefit the organization could have received from a project that was not undertaken.

Explicit Costs

Explicit costs are tangible business expenses. These types of expenses can be accounted for because they involve a cash outlay and can be claimed as business expenses in accounting and tax records. Explicit costs are deducted from revenues when figuring an organization's profitability. Types of explicit costs include wages, office rent, office supplies, costs of goods sold, and legal fees.

Short-Run Costs and Long-Run Costs

Short-run costs are those costs that an organization incurs during a short period of time. This time period does not allow for any variation in the amount of input. Long-run costs are those costs incurred over a longer period of time. Because of this longer time period, the variation in inputs can be varied and such items such as production capacity can be varied.

Economic Profit

Economic profit is total revenues earned less explicit and implicit costs.

Economic profit takes into account the opportunity costs of using an organization's resources on one project instead of using those same resources on another project. Economic profit is not synonymous with accounting profit. Accounting profit does not consider implicit or opportunity costs. In most instances, economic profit is less than or equal to accounting profit.

Plant-Wide Overhead Rate

The plant-wide overhead rate is a method of measuring product costs. The plant-wide overhead rate is an overhead rate that has been predetermined and applies to all departments or processes within an organization. The plant-wide overhead rate is used when all of the departments or processes operate in much the same manner. This results in a cost rate that is uniformly applied to all products.

Fixed and Variable Overhead Expenses

Fixed expenses are those costs that do not change depending on the level of business activity. These costs stay the same when the organization is operating at 100% capacity and when it is not producing any product. Variable expenses are costs that change depending on the level of activity. These costs may increase depending on an increase in production and on changes in production methods.

Overapplied Overhead and Underapplied Overhead

Applied overhead is the factory overhead that has been allocated to all the processes or products of an organization. Applied overhead is calculated as factory overhead plus work-in-process inventory multiplied by a predetermined overhead rate. This overhead is then allocated to cost centers. When the total amount allocated to all cost centers exceeds actual overhead, the result is overapplied overhead. When the total amount allocated to all cost centers is less than the actual overhead, the result is underapplied overhead.

Departmental Overhead Rate

The departmental overhead rate is a method of measuring product costs. The departmental overhead rate is an individual overhead rate for each department or process within an organization. Departmental overhead rates are used when products do not use the same amount of labor resources and labor hours. In these cases, a product may require a large number of labor hours in one department and a smaller amount of labor hours in another department. This may be that in one step of the process or production, the product is labor intensive and, in another step, the product is manufactured with computerized equipment.

Direct Allocation Method

The direct allocation method is a way to distribute the costs incurred by each service department within an organization to the production department that benefited from the service provided. This method does not take into account any services provided for other service departments. This is the most widely used allocation method.

Step-Down Method

The step-down method is a cost allocation method that allocates the cost of services provided by one service department in an organization to other service departments. This allocation involves a sequence of cost allocation events. The service department that provides service to the largest number of other departments will have its costs allocated first and will continue until the service department that provides the least amount of service will have its costs allocated last.

Reciprocal Method

The reciprocal method is a cost allocation method where costs of an organization's service department are allocated to the production departments. This method is used in organizations where there is an agreement between several service departments to share costs. For example, the service department of the Engineering division will add its costs with the service department of the Sales division and the total of these costs are then allocated to the departments, jobs, or processes that used the services.

Just-In-Time Manufacturing System Benefits

There are many benefits to just-in-time systems. By improving its manufacturing process, an organization will be able to identify and address problems, make systems simpler to understand and manage, reduce the amount of time it takes to set up a product for production, provide for efficient flow of material through the manufacturing process, gain greater quality control, and keep machinery and other equipment in good working order. By eliminating waste, the organization will not incur added costs due to overproduction, increased time spent in the manufacturing process, defective product, unnecessary transportation costs, and a higher than needed level of inventory. The greatest benefit to the organization is that by implementing a just-in-time system, the organization will become more competitive within the marketplace.

Purpose of Just-In-Time Manufacturing Systems

The purpose of just-in-time manufacturing systems is a means of producing a product with the least amount of waste in terms of time, resources, and materials. It is also a means to produce an amount of product that will exactly meet customer demands. To obtain this minimum level of waste, an organization must strive to continually improve its manufacturing process, eliminate the inefficient use of time and materials, and promote the practice of workplace cleanliness and organization.

Work Cells

A work cell is a single process in the manufacturing line. Each work cell is assigned two kanbans—a withdrawal kanban and a production-ordering kanban. In this way, each worker in the process knows what materials are needed to complete a job and how much product the worker is expected to produce with these materials. Each work cell is separate from other work cells. Each work cell has a production schedule. In order for the organization to meet its production schedule, changes only need to be made in the final assembly stage if an individual work cell becomes behind schedule. This also helps management identify problem areas and take steps to improve the production process.

Kanban

A kanban is the method used to achieve the production schedule specified by a just-in-time system. A kanban is a card that specifies the order of the manufacturing process. There are withdrawal kanbans and production-ordering kanbans. The withdrawal kanban tells production line workers which product and the amount of product they need from the preceding step in the manufacturing line in order to complete their part of the product manufacture. A production-ordering kanban tells the production line workers what product they need to produce and in what quantity.

Lean Manufacturing

Lean manufacturing is a method of reducing waste within the manufacturing process to help increase efficiency, while just-in-time manufacturing is a strategy to increase efficiency and reduce waste by receiving goods only when they are needed for the production process. Lean manufacturing also focuses on adding value for the customer while being more efficient. There are seven types of waste in manufacturing. They are over production, unnecessary motion, unnecessary inventory, production of defects, waiting, transportation, and inappropriate processing. Another key principle of lean manufacturing is continuous improvement. There is always room for improvement and there should always be changes made to the production process to continue to be more efficient.

Enterprise Resource Planning (ERP)

Enterprise resource planning (ERP) is business management software that is used to help companies collect, store, manage and interpret data from their many business activities. It can be used to track production planning and costs, manufacturing, marketing, sales, inventory, and shipping. ERP benefits businesses by giving them an integrated view of the business process in real-time. They can track important resources such as cash, raw materials, production capacity, orders, and payroll. It is considered a vital tool because of the way it integrates varied organizational systems and facilitates error-free transactions.

Outsourcing

Outsourcing is a method of reducing costs by using outside suppliers to perform a portion of the manufacturing process or other work needed by the organization instead of the organization performing this work using its own work force and facilities. Before considering outsourcing a portion of the work, an organization needs to weigh the benefit of potential cost savings against the disadvantage of potential loss of control over the product produced. To have a successful outsourcing relationship with an outside vendor, the organization must 1) determine what type of outsourcing relationship will best fit its needs, 2) gain the support of its management and staff, 3) use referrals to find potential outsourcing vendors that can meet the organization's needs, 4) perform in-depth research into the abilities of the outsourcing vendors to make sure the vendor can meet the organization's needs, and 5) develop a contract that defines responsibilities, performance goals, confidentiality rules, and ownership rights.

Benefits of Outsourcing

The main reason for outsourcing is to increase profits and efficiency. This can be accomplished by selecting a vendor that can perform the work more efficiently by producing in greater volume. Outsourcing reduces the number of employees needed by the organization and reduces the workload of its current employee base. Outsourcing allows an organization to eliminate work that it does not do well and to focus on those areas it can perform efficiently. By eliminating work that the organization cannot do efficiently, the morale of the organization can be increased. Outsourcing can improve an organization's cash flow and financial stability. Outsourcing vendors may bring additional knowledge and skills to the manufacturing process and the organization. Outsourcing can create a product of higher quality.

Disadvantages of Outsourcing

When an organization outsources a portion of its manufacturing process or other work it loses control over the final product which may result in a product of lower quality. When an organization's final product is inferior, it may result in decreased loyalty from employees and customers. When considering outsourcing, an organization has a time investment involved in finding an outsourcing vendor. There is the research time and the time investing in the bidding process which translates to added costs to the organization.

Theory of Constraints

The theory of constraints was developed by Dr. Eliyahu M. Goldratt. The approach is to look at the entire organization not as a complex system of people and machines but as a large number of small units. This approach intends to simplify the organization's structure and make it easier for the organization to meet its goals. It does this by isolating those units that act as constraints in the organization's system.

The theory of constraints helps an organization run more efficiently and improves its chances of meeting its goals. This allows the organization to increase profits and earn a greater return on its investment. It does this by increasing the efficiency of the manufacturing process and decreases the amount of lead time needed by the production process. It reduces the amount of inventory an organization needs to hold both in work-in-process and finished goods. It makes it easier for the organization to deliver goods on time. It also provides a tool that helps management and staff resolve problems and conflicts.

Drum-Buffer-Rope System

The drum-buffer-rope system is a method used by the theory of constraints to manage the production process. It is based on the assumption that the least capable resource in the production process is the determining factor in setting the production schedule. The least capable resource is called the capacity constraint resource (CCR). The CCR is the resource in the production system that can cause bottlenecks. This CCR is referred to as the drum and it sets the production pace. The rope is the communication mechanism that releases work into the production process at a rate that the CCR can handle. A buffer is between the drum and the rope to ensure that materials are in place and ready to be processed when the CCR is available to do the work. The buffer also ensures that the end product is produced on time so that orders are not delayed.

Throughput

Throughput is the rate at which an organization produces income. Throughput is a tool used by the theory of constraints to break an organization into a large number of money units. It is a financial measurement that helps an organization run more profitably and increases its chances of meeting its goals. Throughput equals sales revenue less the cost of raw materials.

Technology Advances That Aid in Increasing Productivity

Computer aided manufacturing systems automate processes and tasks by applying robotics and computer-aided design. Robotics uses machines to perform jobs, such as welding car doors or packaging candy in boxes. Instead of using employees to perform routine jobs, robots do the repetitive work. Programming your VCR to record your favorite show when you won't be home is another example of robotics and automation. Computer-aided design systems automate the design and development stage of a product's development. The product development process of drawing blueprints, assembling parts lists, and detailing product specifications is made easier because changes can be made quickly. In addition, three-dimensional models can be created and the product's movements can be simulated through animation. Computer-integrated manufacturing uses computer technology so that all parts of an organization can communicate and work efficiently together. Flexible manufacturing systems allow the organization to take corrective action when changes need to be made. It also allows it the time to take corrective action. This may be beneficial when a part of the system is not running at peak performance, or a new product needs to be added to the manufacturing process.

Value Chain Analysis

A value chain is a way of looking at an organization as a series or chain of events that takes inputs (such as materials) and creates an output (or product) that can be delivered to the consumer. Value chain analysis looks at each of the activities or production processes used to create a product that meets the needs of its customers. By analyzing these inputs and outputs, the organization is better able to assess its strengths and weaknesses.

Value chain analysis helps an organization expand by identifying opportunities and threats, by improving the strategic planning system, and by giving the organization access to low cost financing. It helps an organization hire and retain quality employees by providing a reward system and minimizing absenteeism and turnover. It improves the research and development process by supporting innovation and cooperation within the organization. It helps the organization obtain materials on a timely basis, at the least cost, and at the highest quality. It helps the organization improve marketing and sales by identifying market segments, using innovative advertising techniques, finding additional distribution channels, and motivating the sales staff. It also provides a means of providing quality customer service by listening to customers' input and complaints, implementing guarantee and replacement policies, and providing customer education and training.

Value Chain Analysis Steps

First the organization's production process needs to be broken down into unique, individual activities. Once each activity is isolated, the costs associated with the activity can be measured and a budget created. Then, each of the activities is evaluated in terms of how it makes the organization different from its competition. After each activity is evaluated, the entire value chain can be examined to see if there are any areas that could be improved. Finally, the value chain can be compared to the value chains of the organization's competitors.

Pareto Principle

The Pareto principle states that 80% of the consequences derive from 20% of the causes. In other words, a small number of causes in a given population create the largest number of results. For example, 20% of an organization's customers account for 80% of sales revenue. The Pareto principle was originally applied to the distribution of income and wealth within a population. But it can also be applied to quality control and resource optimization methods. In these methods, 20% of the organization's manufacturing processes use 80% of the resources. It is used to optimize the amount of goods an organization keeps on hand and to reduce the costs of holding and replenishing materials needed for production.

Reengineering

Business process reengineering looks at how the organization operates in an attempt to improve efficiency. Its aim is to improve manufacturing processes by decreasing time and minimizing effort. It does this by studying and then designing time-saving tasks and procedures for all areas of the organization. It increases an organization's ability to be competitive by providing quality customer service, a product that meets the needs of the customers and by designing management and manufacturing processes that use the least amount of time and material resources.

Best Practice Analysis

Best practice analysis is the continuous search to improve an organization's processes and procedure. This is done by looking at other organizations that are considered to be the best in the industry. To determine if an organization is doing its best, its key outputs are compared to the outputs of other organizations and the differences are evaluated. If the organization sees that another organization performs a task or procedure better, it can then see if emulating that organization's performance would be beneficial.

Kaizen (Continuous Improvement)

Kaizen is a means to improve an organization's processes by eliminating waste, timing production with customer needs, and standardizing job processes. By improving an organization's processes, the organization can achieve cost reductions within the entire product manufacturing cycle. In addition, kaizen brings efficiency to the workforce by reducing manual labor and teaching employees to accomplish more by eliminating wasted movement and methods. This attention to the efficiency and productivity of the workforce is key to kaizen.

Principles of Total Quality Management (TQM)

Total quality management encompasses the principles of quality, teamwork, proactive management philosophies, and process improvement. When these principles are applied effectively within an organization, there will be a constant and continual increase in the quality of products and services supplied by the organization. These principles are applied in many ways. The first step toward achieving total quality is proper planning, well thought out policies, and effective administration of these plans and policies. Next, products and services produced by the organization should be designed to be efficient and useful. There should also be procedures in place that allow quick and easy methods for design changes. Materials purchased for the use in manufacturing products and providing services should be controlled to keep costs down and quality up. To ensure that the organization is providing a quality product or service, there should be customer contact and product testing. If the product does not perform to expected standards or if costs are not controlled, corrective action needs to be taken. And, finally, to ensure the highest quality product and the most productive manufacturing processes, employees should be selected carefully and a system of training and motivation should be implemented.

Total Quality Management (TQM)

Total quality management is a process where an organization works to improve the quality of its manufacturing processes and of the services it provides. The core of total quality management is obtaining feedback and using that feedback to make continuous improvements to the organization's existing processes. The goal of total quality management is the elimination of defects from the manufacturing process, the elimination of waste from the labor process, and the elimination of waste in the materials used. By eliminating defects and waste, an organization can increase the quality of its products and increase productivity. This in turn will help the organization increase its productivity and competitiveness.

Implementing a Total Quality Management Program

Total quality management programs are implemented in five stages – preparation, planning, assessment, implementation, and diversification. In the preparation stage, the decision is made as to whether or not to start a total quality management program. In this stage, needs are identified, goals are developed, policies are formulated, resources are identified, and goals are communicated to the organization. In the planning stage, the budget and schedule for the program is developed. In addition, resources are committed and the program support plan is put in place. In the assessment stage, input is taken from customer and employees as to the quality of the labor base and the organization. In the implementation stage, training begins so that employees are aware of the program and the role they play in the program. In the diversification stage, outside opinions from suppliers, customers, distributors, and competitors are sought. Also included in this stage are employee training, awards given for excellent performance, and partnership agreements that will further the development of the total quality management program.

Successful Total Quality Management Program Characteristics

In order for a total quality management program to succeed within an organization, the program needs to encompass three important characteristics – participative management, continuous process improvement, and teamwork. Participative management means that every manager and employee within the organization is involved in the management process. Policies and decisions are made with input from those employees that are responsible for the tasks that are guided by the policies and decisions. This motivates employees to perform to their best abilities. Continuous process improvement provides recognition for the smallest gains in productivity and improvement. Not only does this provide motivation to achieve larger, long-term goals, but it requires the organization to look farther into the future. Teamwork involves the sharing of knowledge between departments and employees, the identification of problems and opportunities, and helps employees understand their role in the organization. This motivates employees to work to achieve the goals of the organization.

Control Charts

Control charts are also called Shewhart charts or process-behavior charts. A control chart is one of the seven basic tools of quality control. It is a statistical tool that is used to determine variations in processes and to help in the forecasting and management functions of an organization. The control chart provides a visual method to detect changes or variations in process levels. The control chart consists of a sequence of quantitative data represented within five horizontal lines. A center line is drawn at the process mean point. An upper warning limit line is drawn two standard deviations above the center line. An upper control limit line is draw three standard deviations above the center line. A lower warning limit line is drawn two standard deviations below the center line. A lower control limit line is drawn three standard deviations below the center line. When the data for a process falls outside the limits, then action needs to be taken on that process.

Check Sheets

A check sheet is one of the seven basic tools of quality control. Check sheets are used to collect quantitative and qualitative data. Data is recorded by making check marks on the sheet. There are five types of check sheets. A classification check sheet classifies traits into categories. A location check sheet indicates the physical location of a trait. A frequency check sheet shows the presence or absence of a trait. A measurement scale check sheet displays intervals and measurements that are indicated by checking the appropriate interval. A check list check sheet lists the items to be performed for a task and as the task is complete, the item is checked off.

Use of Histograms

A histogram is one of the seven basic tools of quality control. A histogram is normally displayed as a bar graph that plots the frequency of a number of events. A histogram is a graphical representation of tables. It represents the proportion of events that fall into a defined set of categories. The histogram is a common format for displaying statistical data. It is an easy to interpret format that shows the largest and smallest frequencies. It also gives an indication of the distribution of the data being charted.

Flowcharts

A flowchart is one of the seven basic tools of quality control. Flowcharts are a graphical representation of a sequence of steps that are involved in a task or process. Flowcharts show all of the inputs and outputs involved in the task or process in a logical order. Each step is displayed in its proper order and the relationship between steps is indicated. Each element is indicated as a graphical image. Symbols are used to represent each step and each step is connected with other steps by lines and arrows. Flowcharts can be used to document any task or process from the manufacturing process involved with building a product, how invoices and other paperwork are processed in an organization, and how data is processed from source documents through a computer system.

Pareto Chart

A Pareto chart is one of the seven basic tools of quality control. It is typically a bar chart that contains a left vertical axis and a right vertical axis. The left vertical axis represents a frequency of occurrence, a cost, or another unit of measure. The right vertical axis is the cumulative percentage of the total number of occurrences, the total cost, or the total of the other unit of measure. The purpose of the Pareto chart is to show which factor among a number of factors is the most important. When used in a quality control setting, the Pareto chart will indicate causes of manufacturing defects, types of manufacturing defects, reasons for customer complaints, reasons for manufacturing delays, and reasons for shipping and transportation problems.

Ishikawa Diagrams

An Ishikawa diagram is one of the seven basic tools of quality control. Ishikawa diagrams are also called fishbone diagrams or cause and effect diagrams. Ishikawa diagrams show the causes of an event. These cause and effect diagrams display relationships between variables and the related causes. This is helpful in determining behaviors of associated processes. The causes are divided into categories – the 6 M's, the 8 P's, and the 4 S's. The 6 M's are machine, method, materials, measurement, man, and Mother Nature. These are used in manufacturing environments. The 8 P's are price, promotion, people, processes, places/plant, policies, procedures, and product. These are used for administrative purposes and in service industries. The 4 S's are surroundings, suppliers, systems, and skills. These are used in service industries. Ishikawa diagrams are most often used in product design where developers need to know what factors in the product are desirable.

Internal Control

Internal control is a means that ensures that an organization is operating according to established management practices. The purpose of internal control is to keep track of assets, prevent fraud, reduce errors, and validate financial data. There are two types of internal controls -- accounting controls and administrative controls. Accounting controls ensure that financial records are accurate and that all transactions are properly authorized. Administrative controls assure that the organization is running according to management policies and that the organization is operating efficiently. The most important part of internal control is the internal audit. The audit reports the adequacy of existing controls.

Scatter Diagrams

A scatter diagram is one of the seven basic tools of quality control. Scatter diagrams are used to establish a relationship between two sets of measurements. A scatter diagram uses a graph format where dots are placed at data points that represent. One measurement is displayed on the vertical axis and the other measurement is displayed on the horizontal axis. When the dots form a diagonal line, there is an association between the two sets of measurements. The relationship can be either positive (a rising line that slopes from the lower left corner to the upper right corner of the graph), negative (a falling line that slopes from the upper left corner to the lower right corner of the graph), or no relationship.

Efficient Accounting Practices

Many accounting firms underutilize their accounting software. They don't take the time to learn the full functionality of the system and end up taking a lot longer than needed to get work done. If necessary, consider hiring someone to come in and train the staff on all of the functions. It is important to review your accounting processes from time to time as they can become outdated and inefficient. After this is it may be necessary to send employees to training. These classes can help with professional development, provide systems training, and help with just general day-to-day activities.

Business Process Analysis

Business process analysis breaks down a procedure in a step-by-step approach. It analyzes the phases of each part of a process by looking at the inputs, operations, and output. By analyzing a business process, you gain a greater understanding of how it works. Steps that create areas of waste or weakness can be identified, as well as opportunities to improve the overall efficiency and effectiveness of the process.

After selecting the process to be analyzed, information is collected that will help gain an understanding as to its inputs and outputs. Once data is gathered, the steps are mapped out in a visual format which clearly shows how the process is conducted from start to finish. From there, critical steps should be analyzed for areas that may indicate a weakness or inefficiency, as well as potential opportunities to improve its effectiveness or efficiency.

A business process consists of a series of steps that an organization takes to create a product or carry out its service. The way in which an organization carries out its business processes can directly impact its profitability. Efficient and effective processes make the best use of a company's resources, which can result in higher profits and value. A company can improve its business process thru;

- Process analysis involves breaking it down into the steps that it takes to complete it from start to finish. These steps are often listed out sequentially in a visual format, such as a flowchart. These steps can be evaluated to identify waste or weakness. You can also identify areas of opportunity that can improve overall efficiency and effectiveness.

Example: If a company uses multiple stand-alone software systems to complete its tasks, employees may waste time inputting the same information in multiple places. An opportunity for improvement may exist if the company implements an enterprise resource planning system (ERP) that connects multiple business processes and automates the flow of information between them, thus reducing the need for duplicate data entry.

- When a company identifies areas of weakness, the process can be redesigned to eliminate excess waste or cost. Similarly, a redesigned process can help a company take advantage of opportunities to improve its efficiency and effectiveness.
  Example: The use of one centralized printer in an office can save a company money, however, if office personnel are constantly leaving their desk on a regular basis to pick up their print jobs, it may wasting more resources through lost time and employee distractions. A potential redesign of the process be to place multiple printers throughout the office or giving each employee their own desktop printer. This can reduce the distance that an employee has to travel to pick up their print job and reduce the impact to their efficiency every time they leave their desk.
- Standardization allows a company to create a uniform approach to its process. By choosing the best way to complete tasks and implementing this approach across the organization, overall efficiency will improve.

By analyzing a process, redesigning its steps to address waste or incorporate areas of opportunity, and creating a standardized approach to carry out its process, a company can improve its overall business process.

Business Process Standardization

Business process standardization creates a unified and consistent approach to completing a task. It starts by analyzing the steps of a specific process and creating a visual picture to reflect the flow of the process from start to finish. When areas of weakness or opportunities for efficiency are identified, the step can be redesigned.

Standardization is similar to creating a "best practices" approach whereby the company documents how a process should be carried out across the organization. It requires the company to determine the most efficient and effective way to complete a process and ensures that everyone in the company is aware of the practice.

There are many benefits to process standardization. These include:

- Choose the best way – When an organization determines the most efficient way to complete the process and implements a standard approach across all departments, overall efficiency will improve.
- Employee learning – It will be easier for new employees to learn a process when one approach is documented and taken.
- Easier to troubleshoot – If all employees follow the same standard approach, it will be easier for an organization to identify a problem in the process itself. When various approaches are followed to complete the same task, the organization will need to consider if the problem exists in the process or the way in which it is being carried out.

Internal Controls

Components of Internal Control

Internal control consists of a control environment, risk assessment, control activities, information, and monitoring. The control environment provides a structure for employee integrity, organizational competence, management operating style, and oversight by the board of directors. Risk assessment is the identification, analysis, and management of uncertainty meeting the organization's financial, compliance, and operational objectives. Control activities are the policies and procedures maintained by an organization that address risk areas and safeguards against wrong actions. Information is the identification, collection, and exchange of financial, operational, and compliance information in a timely manner. Monitoring is the assessment of the quality of internal controls. Monitoring provides information about problem areas a control system.

Aim of Internal Control

Internal control is the sum set of processes for a company which is designed to improve the company's objectives regarding the reliability of their financial statements, the efficacy and efficiency of their business activities, and the conformity of their practices with established legislation, with the emphasis especially placed upon financial statement reliability. Since the possibility of conspiracy, management override, or innocent errors in judgment or application may arise in any system, it is important to remember that the goal of internal control is not to eliminate all chances of error, but to reasonably limit them. Management is ultimately responsible for internal control effectiveness.

Maintaining Internal Control

Everyone associated with an organization is responsible for maintaining internal control, but most of the responsibility is with management, the board of directors, internal auditors, and external auditors. Management is responsible for the annual financial report to shareholders and for maintaining the internal control system. The board of directors is responsible for making sure the internal control system is effective. The internal auditors ensure the adequacy of the internal control system, the reliability of the data, and the efficient use of resources. The external auditors report any internal control weaknesses.

Internal Control Risk

Internal control risk is a risk that a material error can occur in the financial records of an organization. The risk is that the error will not be detected by the internal controls of the organization or that it will not be prevented. To ensure adequate control, an organization will need to implement a system where duties are segregated between employees, where there is a system of checks and verifications, that high-quality personnel are hired, that the duties and relationships of employees are detailed, and that internal audits are effective.

Organizational Structure

The organizational structure of an organization determines the line of authority. It shows which subordinates are accountable to which supervisors. The organizational structure shows the chain of command and the individual responsible for final approval on all decisions. The organizational structure also defines guidelines for how work is to be completed and the individual responsible for each stage of the work. The purpose of an organizational structure is to ensure communication between employees and coordination between work projects.

> **Review Video: Corporate Organizational Structure**
> Visit mometrix.com/academy and enter code: 752986

Importance of Policies and Procedures

Policies and procedures are written instructions that describe how an organization operates. Written policies and procedures include a purpose statement, a list of individuals affected by the policy and procedure, the scope of the procedure, definitions of terms used in the policy or procedure, and the individuals responsible for implementing and maintaining the procedure. Policies and procedures make sure that the organization operates within applicable laws and that the operation runs efficiently. Policies and procedures also give auditors a mechanism to ensure that controls are in place and working correctly.

Board of Director's Responsibilities to Shareholders

The primary concern of any corporation is that all business decisions should consider the effects on the organization's shareholders. The shareholders should be considered first in the decision-making process. Any decision needs to determine whether or not there will be an effect on the dividends, interest, and capital gains paid to shareholders.

Components of Audit Risk

Audit risk is the risk that an auditor will provide an inappropriate opinion as to whether or not the financial statements of an organization clearly represent the financial position of the organization. The components of audit risk are inherent risk, control risk, and detection risk. Inherent risk does not take internal controls into consideration. It is only a measure of whether or not there may be material misstatements in the financial statements. Control risk is a measure that misstatements will not be prevented or detected by the internal control system. Detection risk is the risk that an auditor will not find a material misstatement in the unaudited information.

Segregation of Duties

Segregation of duties is an internal control method where responsibility for activities is shared between several employees. Segregation of duties keeps errors to a minimum and reduces improper actions by employees. Segregation of duties occurs when the record keeping function for an asset is performed by one employee and the management of the assets is performed by another employee. Keeping the approval of payments separate from the writing and signing of checks is another example of segregation of duties.

Responsibilities of Independent Auditors

Independent auditors must comply with six ethical principles of professional conduct. They are to exercise professional and moral judgments in all their actions. They are to act in the public interest. They are to perform their work with a high level of integrity. They are to be free of conflicts of interest when performing professional services. They are to observe the profession's technical and ethical standards. They are to observe these principles of the Code of Professional Conduct when determining the scope and nature of the services to be provided.

Title II, Title III, and Section 303 of the Sarbanes-Oxley Act (SOX)

Besides establishing the PCAOB, which is itself overseen by the SEC, the Sarbanes-Oxley Act (SOX) seeks to preserve auditor independence by forbidding registered public accounting firms from additionally giving certain nonaudit services to their clients, including bookkeeping services, design for financial information systems, appraisal or valuation, actuarial services, internal audit outsourcing services, management or human resources, financial services, legal services, and others.

SOX also requires that audit committees for client companies be in charge of hiring and overseeing the work of external audit companies, including the preapproval of permissible nonaudit activities by the external audit company.

Role of Shareholders, the Board of Directors, and Officers

Shareholders have the right to corporation information; if shareholders have a proper purpose, they have the right to inspect the corporation books.

Shareholders must approve the following decisions: dissolution, mergers, charter or bylaw amendments, or sale of assets.

Corporations are generally run by a board of directors, who are elected by the shareholders. The board of directors is responsible for appointing officers of the corporation. The officers are responsible for running the daily business of the corporation.

Authority and Obligations of the Board of Directors and Officers

Any publicly-traded company is regulated by the SEC and required to have a board of directors, which have the authority and responsibility to oversee the company's operations, including not only its profit-generating strategy but its financial accountability to the public. Consequently, the board of directors ought to have a variety of people with expertise in financial reporting and in the business's operations, as well as an overall awareness of all the stakeholders' interests in the company's reporting and operations.

Officers hold similar levels of authority and responsibility. Major officers are generally appointed by an entity's board of directors. They can be officers and directors simultaneously, and they are also permitted to serve in more than one office.

Audit Committee

An audit committee is a committee independent of the corporation, but composed of board members, which is responsible for the audit work performed by the company's internal auditors and external auditors. Internal auditors have to directly report to the audit committee. At least one member of the audit committee must be a financial expert. Sarbanes-Oxley also establishes many regulations concerning the responsibilities and authority of audit committees.

Disclosure Committee

Disclosure committees are not required to be formed, but are helpful in dealing with a company's disclosure issues. Such committees would help to determine the materiality of information and the applicability of certain disclosure requirements, improve company processes to ensure that quality information is disclosed in a timely manner, and assist with other disclosure issues. Disclosure committees typically report to the chief executives of the corporation.

Company's Responsibilities Pertaining to an External Auditor

Since an external auditor ought to remain independent both in fact and in appearance, it is likewise vital that the company not compromise his independence in any way. This fundamentally involves the company taking responsibility for the appropriate activities and the external auditor taking responsibility for the appropriate activities. For example, the external auditor cannot be responsible about the effectiveness of the company's internal controls; that is the management's responsibility. According to the SEC, external auditors are permitted to gather information about a company, but management must direct the information-gathering process. If the auditor were solely in charge of both collecting information and appraising how well it was collected, it could too easily be interpreted as the auditor's auditing his own work.

Control Environment

The control environment reflects the overall attitude, awareness, and actions of the board of directors, management, owners, and others concerning the importance of control and its emphasis in the entity.

Factors which collectively affect the control environment include:

1. Integrity and ethical values – code of conduct, use of appropriate incentive schemes
2. Audit committee and Board of Directors – oversee accounting policies and practices
3. Philosophy of management and operating style – attitude toward financial reporting, approach to risk
4. Assignment of authority and responsibility
5. Commitment to competence – ensuring competence, requisite skills, knowledge for particular jobs
6. Human resource policies and procedures – sufficient, competent personnel with adequate resources
7. Organizational structure – assigns authority and responsibility

Relevance of the Sarbanes-Oxley Act (SOX) to Internal Control

The Sarbanes-Oxley Act requires companies to establish and maintain an appropriate system of internal control.

Section 302 of the act requires a company's chief officers to review and certify the financial statements' accuracy, reliability, and completeness, as well as the internal controls' reliability and effectiveness. Signing officers have a very high liability according to SOX in order to motivate them to personally ensure the reliability of the controls and financial statement assertions.

Section 404 demands that management also work for the implementation and maintenance of an appropriate control structure.

Types of Audit Reports

There are five types of audit reports. The unqualified opinion is used when the financial statements fairly represent the organization's financial position, results of operations, and cash flows in accordance with GAAP. The unqualified opinion with explanatory language is used when the financial statements comply with GAAP but there has been a change in accounting practices. The qualified opinion is used when the auditor feels that there has been a material departure from GAAP in the organization's accounting practices. The adverse opinion is used when the auditor feels that the financial statements do not fairly present the organization's financial position, results of operations, and cash flows. The disclaimer of opinion is used when the auditor cannot determine whether or not the financial statements present the organization's financial position, results of operations, and cash flows.

Information Provided to an Organization by Internal Auditors

An internal audit discloses how well an organization is doing at meeting its goals and complying with laws and regulations. An internal auditor determines if sound procurement practices have been followed, if resources have been properly maintained and utilized, if there is any duplication of effort in the organization, if operating procedures are efficient and are being followed, and if there is an adequate management control system.

Operational Audit

An operational audit is an evaluation of how well the management of an organization has conformed to organizational policies and budgets. The objective of an operational audit is to see how well an organization is meeting its goals. It measures management's effectiveness and efficiency.

Compliance Audit

A compliance audit determine whether or not an organization is following the laws, regulations, policies and procedures set by regulators and the organization's written policies. It is the auditor's responsibility to determine that internal controls are being adhered to. The auditor writes a report stating the condition of the internal controls and makes recommendations for improvement. It is also the job of the auditor to determine if the organization is complying with applicable laws and regulations.

Purpose of the Public Company Accounting Oversight Board (PCAOB)

The Public Company Accounting Oversight Board is responsible for the regulation of auditors of publicly traded companies. It was created as a result of the Sarbanes-Oxley Act of 2002. Its goal is to protect shareholders and ensure that an organization's financial statements follow specified guidelines. The PCAOB has several responsibilities as defined by the Sarbanes-Oxley Act. It registers and inspects public accounting firms and initiates disciplinary actions when needed. It also sets auditing, quality control, ethics, and other standards for audit reports.

Purpose of Quality Audits and Gap Analyses

Quality audits are an examination of a quality system. Quality audits are executed on a regular basis to ensure that an organization complies with its internal quality monitoring procedures and takes corrective action when standards are not met. When performing a quality audit, the auditor reviews the standard operating procedures to make sure they comply with the applicable regulations. The auditor also analyzes the actual processes and compares the results with the standard operating procedures. Gap analysis is an assessment tool that allows an organization to compare actual performance against potential performance. The goal is to improve how efficiently resources are used. Gap analysis looks at the resources used and the organization's potential, records how resources are used, and determines the organization's optimum resource usage. The organization's capabilities are compared to the average performance of other organizations within the industry. This gives the organization a realistic idea of the performance level it wants to achieve in the future.

Information Systems Threats

Computer information systems can be vulnerable to a variety of threats. Input manipulation, program alteration, direct file alteration, data theft, sabotage, viruses, Trojan horses, and theft are the most common threats. A Trojan horse is a self-replicating program virus. A Trojan horse makes changes in computer systems. It can also replicate itself and infect other software applications or computers. Viruses and Trojan horses are some of the hardest threats to deal with. They can quickly find their way into a computer system and do their damage before their devastation is noticed.

Role Information Technology Plays in the Internal Control Process

Most organizations use computers to keep financial data, documents, and other important information. Most corporations have an information officer that is responsible for the security, accuracy, and reliability of these computer systems and the data contained in them. Because this information is vital to the reporting of financial data, these systems need to be assessed for security risks so that the data is not compromised.

Limited Access to Physical Hardware

A number of security mechanisms can be attached to a piece of computer hardware. These devices include locks and fingerprint identification pads. These devices are intended to discourage theft. Software controls that prohibit unauthorized users from gaining access to the computer are network vulnerability scanning and firewalls. Network vulnerability scanning continually tests the level of protection at all access points into the system. A firewall controls access between the protected system and outside systems. A firewall limits both incoming and outgoing transmissions.

Steps to Achieve Control over Information Systems

Before a control system can be developed for an information system, any activities that pose a risk to the completeness and accuracy of financial reports must be discovered. Next, employees need to be trained in the proper use of information technology. Then, a system needs to be designed that ensures accurate reporting of financial information. In addition, written policies should be developed so that errors and misunderstandings are minimized. Once the system is in place, it needs to be monitored and audited to make sure that high risk areas are properly handled.

Input Control

Input controls ensure that data input into a system is kept secure. Input controls include methods to make sure that data input into the system is from an authorized user, that it is a proper electronic format, and that data has not been lost or improperly changed.

Output Control

Output controls make sure that the data displayed is correctly. The data display includes any data the is displayed on a computer monitor or on a printer, reports that are generated, files that are downloaded, and other information that is processed in some manner. Output controls also ensure that the user who accesses the information is authorized to do so.

Processing Control

Processing controls ensure that applications perform as expected. Processing controls make sure that data is processed by authorized users, that all data is accounted for, and that no unauthorized data is input into the system. Processing control keeps data on the system and ensures that the data is accurate and not changed by unauthorized use.

Software Programs and Databases Unauthorized Use Protection

Computer access in an organization should be limited to authorized users. To keep software systems and data secure, a method to control access and identify users must be put in place. To control access, each authorized user is given permission to use the system. This permission is in the form of a username and password that the user enters when accessing the system. As a further measure of security, each authorized user is limited to the data that can be accessed. This type of permission is linked to individual data files, not to the system. Another way to protect data is encryption. Encryption is used when data files are transferred over a network. Encryption makes it difficult for unauthorized users to see the data as it travels between computers on a network or over the Internet.

Internet Use Risks

The Internet is subject to viruses, Trojan horses, and other malicious applications. Data sent over the Internet can be made available to any hacker that can find or follow the information. When using secured transmission lines, the data is either encrypted or only available to users that have the correct username and password. Secured transmission lines limit access to information that is being transmitted over the network.

Storage Controls Used to Keep Data Secure

The best type of storage control is regular data backups. The type of data that should be backed up includes financial data, correspondence, other organizational information, custom software applications, and software device drivers and utilities. This data can be stored on a variety of media including tape or CD-ROM. Backups should be done on a daily or at least weekly basis. The backups should also be stored in several places. One that is easy to get to which may be on the organization's premises. The other backup should be stored at a remote location so that it is protected from damage.

Firewall

A firewall is a method that prevents unauthorized users from gaining access to a computer or a network. Firewalls allow authorized users to access an organization's network or the Internet in a secure and safe manner. Firewalls may also prevent anyone using an organization's computers from accessing other computers on the organization's network or from accessing computers outside the network. A firewall can be either a dedicated piece of computer hardware or a software application.

Data Encryption

Data encryption is a way to make data unavailable to unauthorized users. Encryption turns data into code that cannot be read by an unauthorized user. Before data is sent over the network, it is encrypted (or manipulated) so that it does not resemble the original data. When the data gets to its destination, it is decrypted. This process is accomplished by using either public key or private key technology. The key is the information needed to encrypt and decrypt the message.

Business Continuity Planning (BCP)

Business continuity planning (BCP) is the process by which an organization identifies threats and uses both hard and soft assets to provide prevention and recovery. A BCP is a plan to keep a company operational in case it is affected by some adverse physical condition such as a storm, fire, or crime. The plan should explain how the business would recover from such a disaster. This may include a temporary relocation or a permanent relocation, depending on the severity of the disaster. Other threats to be prepared for are utility outages and cyber attacks. These may be less severe than the others but there still needs to be a plan in place to be able to react to them.

Disaster Recovery Plan

A good disaster recovery plan needs to take many factors into account. A method of contacting the key employees and assigning tasks so that the recovery process can begin as soon as possible after the disaster is needed to get the organization up and running. A backup routine needs to be established to keep sensitive data safe. The organization needs to find a site where operations can be resumed if the original facilities are damaged.

Technology and Analytics

Information Systems

Accounting Information Systems

An accounting information system is a collection of steps used to obtain, retain, manage, process, retrieve, and report financial data. The accounting information system typically relies on software to gather and process data.

The accounting information system facilities interdepartmental activities by linking the related functions within an organization and allowing for the flow of data to occur between them.

Example: As a salesperson completes a sale and enters the invoice into the accounting information system, the purchasing department would automatically receive a requisition for the inventory needed to complete the sale. If the inventory is purchased, the warehouse would be automatically notified of the impending receipt of inventory. When the inventory is received, the warehouse would fill the order and accounts payable would be notified of the amount due. The warehouse would ship the order and the accounts receivable department would be notified to bill the customer.

Internal Controls

Internal controls protect accounting information by limiting access to authorized users. Internal controls are implemented in an accounting information system through the use of passwords, data encryption, role-based employee access rights, and the tracking of system access by employees through computer logs and surveillance. Virus protection, data backup, and network security are used to protect accounting information from unauthorized outside access.

Components

An accounting information system is made up of six components which are:

- The people who use the accounting information system
- The procedures that define how information is collected, stored, disseminated, and analyzed
- The information that is used within the accounting information system
- The software programs that are used to process the data
- The hardware components used to operate the accounting information system
- The internal controls in place to secure and protect the data

Enterprise Resource Planning Systems

An enterprise resource planning system is a series of software applications that connect multiple business processes, which allows for the flow of data between them. By accumulating transactional data from a variety of sources into one centralized system, the enterprise resource planning system connects people and processes across an organization.

An enterprise resource planning system benefits an organization by allowing it to operate more efficiently. By collecting information from multiple sources and depositing the data into one central location, it can eliminate duplicate data. It allows for greater efficiency by automating the sharing of relevant information and tasks between departments, reducing the need to manually enter data into the software, and streamline the business process by making information readily available. An enterprise resource planning system fosters departmental collaboration. The data in an enterprise resource planning system is updated in real-time, which ensures that the most current information is used for sharing and decision-making.

SaaS

Software as a Service, or SaaS, is a collection of remote servers that are located in the cloud. By maintaining the enterprise resource planning system offsite instead of on in-house servers, the Organization can reduce costs by eliminating the need for expensive hardware and additional IT staff. The SaaS provider will manage the software and install patches and upgrades. The Organization will have real-time access to data and can reinvest the cost savings into other areas.

Data Governance

Data Policies and Procedures

Data governance is an overall plan that documents how an organization will manage its data. The plan will include the practices and processes that should be followed to maintain control over its data assets. It is an all-encompassing plan that will detail the methods and behaviors around the stewardship of data, as well the appropriate technologies and processes to ensure the proper level of data quality.

A data governance plan will incorporate key components over the management of its data including:

- Data integrity
- Data usability
- Data availability

Data governance will also include the policies and practices to ensure that data is secure and meets privacy requirements. The plan will also establish the appropriate procedures and policies for employee access, as well as their roles and responsibilities. The plan also incorporates policies and procedures to ensure that the organization meets rules or laws that govern the compliance over data, including access and privacy.

Data governance establishes the framework that an organization follows to manage data throughout its life cycle. Data policies and procedures are put in place to support the overall data governance program.

- Data policies support governance by defining the overall strategies, objectives, and philosophies that should be followed. They are typically broad statements and do not change on a regular basis.
- Procedures document how tasks are carried out. They have a start and a finish. A procedure will have a desired outcome, therefore strict adhere is necessary. They are more descriptive in nature and often follow a step-by-step approach. Procedures may change on a regular basis as-needed. Procedures help to develop uniformity throughout an organization as employees and processes will follow a predetermined approach.

Data policies and procedures work together to accomplish the overall goals of a data governance program. For example, an organization may implement a data backup policy that defines the required frequency and storage location. A backup procedure would document the step-by-step approach to be taken when backing up data and storing it. Combined, the data policy and procedure would support the overall data governance plan's goal of managing its data throughout its lifecycle.

Life Cycle of Data

As data travels through an organization's system, it will go through a variety of steps starting with its inception, usage, and destruction. This is known as the life cycle of data.

The key steps in the life cycle of data include;

- Capture – The first stage in the life cycle of data starts with acquiring data. An enterprise typically obtains its data through;
  - The origination of data from outside of the organization, such as when an order placed on a company's website
  - Data is physically entered into the system. This may occur if a customer calls in and places an order over the phone with a representative
  - From outside devices
- Maintenance – Data maintenance includes all steps necessary to make it ready for use. This includes data cleansing, processing, integration, transformation, and enrichment.
- Usage – When data is applied to tasks that are necessary for an enterprise to operate, this is data usage.
- Publication – This occurs when data is sent outside of the organization. One of the most common forms of publication are reports, such as bank statements.
- Archive – When data reaches the point that it is archived, it is nearing the end of its useful life. At this point, data will be archived, or saved, to a location where no production will occur. Should the data become useful again
- Purge – Data that has reached the end of its useful life will be removed. This is typically done from archived files.

Controls Against Security Breaches

A data security control is designed to keep sensitive data secure and prevent the unauthorized access or use of data. Data security controls can be preventative, detective, or corrective. Organizations use a combination of these controls to prevent security breaches.

- Preventative – These controls are implemented to prevent the loss of data. Common preventative controls include authentication using two factors, limiting employee access and use privilege to the least amount necessary for them to do their job, and use of the cloud.
- Detective – These controls identify areas of weakness where data can be accessed or deleted without authorization. Examples of detective controls include the review of computer logs, continuous monitoring, and an internal audit function. These detective controls are intended to identify actual or potential areas of data loss.
- Corrective – When an actual or potential risk has been identified, a corrective control is implemented to fix the problem. A corrective control may consist of updating a policies and procedures manual or it may be enforcing the current policies in place.

Technology-Enabled Finance Transformation

System Development Life Cycle

A system development life cycle (SDLC) is the process that occurs between the start and completion of a project. The SDLC can be applied to computer projects that emphasize hardware, software, or a combination of both. It takes a comprehensive approach that focuses on the requirements of the end-user and the technologies, policies, and procedures needed to meet these needs.

This development life cycle is comprised of a series of stages which include planning, system analysis, design, system development, testing and implementation, and maintenance. The SDLC uses an iterative approach whereby simple processes are tested first. Results from these iterative tests are reviewed, the processes are updated as needed, and then the test is applied to a larger section of the system. Testing and improvements will continue until the entire system has been tested.

Under the SLDC, security over software applications and computer hardware are considered throughout the entire process. It allows a system to integrate security throughout its stages of development. This eliminates the need to incorporate security features after the project has been completed.

The system development life cycle consists of a series of stages that define and guide the process of completing a computer hardware, software, or combined hardware/software project. The stages of a system development life cycle include:

- Planning – This phase involves identifying what objectives you are trying to accomplish and any problems that you are looking to solve. This stage typically includes identifying available options such as building a new system, improving the existing system, or leaving the current system in place.
- Analysis – Once end-user objectives have been identified, the project should be analyzed for its overall feasibility. Economic, social, and technological factors should be evaluated to determine if it makes sense to move forward with this project.
- Design – Simply put, this phase designs what the system will look like and how it will work. It details the necessary components, architecture, interfaces, security level, and the data that will flow through the system.
- Development – At this stage, the system is built based upon the prescribed design. Software is developed and hardware is configured at this phase.
- Testing and implementation – During this phase, the system is tested using multiple inputs. System outputs are reviewed to determine if it's running properly. The testing phase can be done using live end-users or in-house. The system is implemented according to its intended purpose at this time.
- Maintenance – Systems should be continually reviewed for necessary updates, changes, or upgrades.

PROCESS AUTOMATION

Automation uses technology to perform tasks in a prescribed, sequential manner. The aim is to reduce the need for human involvement in order to improve the efficiency of a process.

Automation allows a company to streamline what it does in order to process only the tasks needed. Reducing unnecessary steps increasing efficiency, thus saving time and costs. Standardizing the processes through automation helps companies who are subject to compliance requirements.

Process automation can be achieved by the following:

- Identification – Companies should review all steps necessary to complete a task. Steps that are considered routine or may be duplicated in other areas should be evaluated as potential candidates for process automation. Identify areas that could benefit from process automation

- Goals – A company should determine what it intends to accomplish by process automation. This could be a reduction in shipping times or increasing access to consistent customer data across multiple departments. Knowing what goals you are looking to achieve will help create effective process automation.
- Map out the process – By mapping out the workflow in a visual manner, such as a flowchart, all steps in the task are identified. The workflow should also identify the employees involved and timeline to complete the tasks
- Key performance indicators (KPIs) – Through KPIs, the efficiency and effectiveness of process automation can be tracked. KPIs are quantifiable measures that a company can use to monitor the success of the process automation. For example, a company that automates its shipping processes may use a KPI to track the reduction in delivery times.
- Test – The system of process automation should be thoroughly tested to ensure that it is functioning according to the mapped workflow and meeting initial KPIs. Flaws or inconsistencies in the system should be addressed before incorporating the automated process into the company's daily activities.

Robotic Process Automation

Robotic process automation (RPA) applies technology, logic, and defined inputs to automate a business process. To achieve RPA, a company sets up its software to

- Interpret the proper application for a transaction
- Process the data according to the application's parameters
- Generate a response to how that data should be used and where it should be sent

An RPA can be as simple as an automated email response to a customer's request through a website. It can also be as complex as a bank using a series of bots programmed to process different claims using set parameters and forwarding them to the appropriate department.

There are several benefits to RPA. These include:

- Reduction of human error, which increases the overall efficiency of a business process
- Less need for staffing to complete tasks, which lowers overall costs
- Bots are also easy to set up and typically don't require significant system integration or specialized software. Not only does this keep overall costs lower, using bots can be easy to implement.
- RPA can also be used in processes that rely on more advanced technologies, such as speech recognition and natural language processing. This allows for greater automation of more complex tasks that typically required human judgment.

Effect of Technology on Processing Accounting Data

Advanced technology has improved the overall efficiency and effectiveness of processing accounting data and information in multiple ways including:

- Artificial intelligence (AI) – AI is a series of computer systems that simulate human intelligence to perform tasks. AI benefits the processing of accounting data and information in many ways including:
  - AI allows for the easy and consistent processing of routine accounting data and information. This can aid in tasks that require compliance as everything is processed in the same way. With a high degree of accuracy, reports generated using accounting data and information are more reliable as there is less chance for error.

    - AI can learn from experience. Taking what it learns from processing accounting data and information, AI can make predictive decisions as to where certain items, such as expenses, should be posted. It can quickly process data and target abnormalities in the information that it receives.
- Robotics – Through the use of programmable bots, processes that typically require human interaction can be automated. The bots work with artificial intelligence to facilitate the month-end closing process, accounts payable and receivable processing, and managing expenses.
- Cloud computing – Cloud computing uses remote servers to store, process, and manage data. There are no delays in accessing information as an end-user can get to their data wherever an internet connection is available. Since all information is housed in one location and uses the same software applications, everyone works with the same data and uses the same tools to do their job. This helps to prevent data duplication and end-users using different programs to do the same thing.

Cloud Computing

Cloud computing refers to a system of remote servers that are hosted through the Internet and are designed to retrieve, process, and store data offsite, instead of on a local computer or server. Cloud computing can improve overall efficiency in a variety of ways including;

- Easy to access – As long as you have an internet connection, cloud computing allows end-users to access their data from any device. This can improve overall efficiency if you are working with multiple devices or have people working from multiple locations. Rather than needing to wait to get to the office to access information, it can easily be done from a laptop, tablet, or smartphone.
- Security – Data that is stored on remote servers through the cloud is subject to strict security measures that you may not typically have on local servers. Robust data encryption and dual log-in authentication processes help to improve the integrity of accounting data and prevent unauthorized access.
- Backup – Data maintained on remote servers is backed up on a regular basis and is often housed in multiple secure facilities in different geographic locations. This can help to ensure that data is not lost in the event of a fire or natural disaster.
- Automatic updates – Accounting firms that use applications that are subject to regulatory changes will always use the most current version available if it's cloud-based. This helps prevent errors in how data is processed.
- Location – By housing all data and applications in one place, all end-users are using the same information. There is less risk for duplication.

Software-as-a-Service

Software-as-a-service (SaaS) is often referred to as "on-demand" software. It is typically hosted in a central location and is licensed for use on a subscription basis. SaaS is typically hosted in the cloud and can be accessed through a web browser. It makes up one of the three cloud-computing categories which also includes platform as a service (PaaS) and Infrastructure as a Service (IaaS).

There are two types of SaaS: Vertical and horizontal. Vertical SaaS are tailored to specific industries such as healthcare, finance, and real estate. Horizontal SaaS relates to a business process or a department, such as accounting, marketing, and human resources.

There are several advantages to SaaS including:

- Scalability – There is a great deal of flexibility with SaaS solutions. Companies can typically add or reduce the number of user licenses that it needs according to their needs.
- Accessibility – Since SaaS is hosted in the cloud, it can be easily accessed with an internet connection and a browser. Depending upon the program, it may also be accessed on multiple devices including personal computers, laptops, smartphones, and iPads.
- Updates – The SaaS provider handles all software and hardware updates which eliminates the need for the company to do this.
- Easy to start – The SaaS solution is already set up in the cloud-based environment, which reduces the start-up time for a customer to use the software.
- Cost-effective – Since SaaS solutions are cloud-based, it eliminates the need for companies to have costly servers and hardware maintenance. Since they are subscription-based, companies typically make monthly payments. This can reduce the overall up-front costs that a company may be required to make.

There are a handful of disadvantages to using SaaS, which are:

- Security – Since a company's data is stored in the cloud, they place a high reliance on the SaaS provider to have effective backup and security protocols in place to prevent data loss and unauthorized access.
- Accessibility – If a company has a poor or unreliable internet connection or experiences an outage, this can impact their ability to access the software.
- Dependency – When a company uses a SaaS solution, they become dependent upon a third party. Should the vendor experience outages or become unreliable in their service, this can impact a company's ability to operate.
- May be limited in functionality – While SaaS solutions continue to evolve, they don't always have the same functionality as a program that you might install on a computer.

DATA ANALYTICS

STRUCTURED, SEMI-STRUCTURED, AND UNSTRUCTURED DATA

Big Data consists of large volumes of data accumulated at a rapid speed. There is a wide variety of big data, including structured, unstructured, and semi-structured. Business enterprises use each type in many ways such as:

- Structured – Also known as relational data, it is the easiest to process because it accumulates in a column and row format. It can be easily mapped into pre-determined fields, which makes it easy to collect, process, and analyze. Some of the most common sources of structured data include spreadsheets, SQL databases, medical devices, and sensors. Business enterprises most commonly use structured data due to its easy access and ability to search. Given its relational database setup, structured data is used by business enterprises to analyze data and make decisions.
- Unstructured – Unstructured data is collected from a variety of sources that is not in a pre-defined or pre-determined format. This lack of consistency makes it harder to accumulate or maintain a relational database on its own. Sources of unstructured data include websites, memos, and videos. While it can be challenging to gather, process, and store, unstructured data is flexible and can be used in a variety of analytical and business intelligence applications.

- Semi-structured – This data does not follow a traditional column and row format; however, some data retains qualities that make it easy to store it in a relational database. Semi-structured data has characteristics of both structured and unstructured data. Sources of semi-structured data include e-mails, zipped files, webpages, and XML.

Data Progression

Data progression reflects the system that data is collected, processed, evaluated, and acted on. Data progression typically follows the Data-Information-Knowledge-Wisdom (DIKW) hierarchy. Each level builds on the initial data received and the previous step by adding value. Data progression starts with;

- Accumulation of data – Data acquired can be in the form of numbers, figures, facts, and text. It can come from multiple sources such as spreadsheets, websites, e-mails, and surveys. As the data is cleaned, processed, and enriched, it moves on to the next stage.
- Process information – Data undergoes processing at this stage. It can include such steps as corroborating relationships between sets of data and verifying its accuracy. Review data at this stage to determine its relevance. Effective data processing adds value to the original data.
- Knowledge – Once data is gathered and processed, the next step to gain an understanding as to what the information reveals. Analyzing the relationships and determining the relevance of the data to a company's goals is a necessary step.
- Insight – By analyzing the relationships, both explicit and implicit, a company can gain greater insight into such things as operations and consumer preferences.
- Action - Through the knowledge and insight gained from the previous steps, a business can make better decisions about its activities, market trends, and customer preferences. A business enterprise can take actionable steps to apply this insight.

Managing Data Analytics

Analyzing raw data to find relevant relationships, identify trends, gain insight, and reach conclusions from the information obtained is known as data analytics. Companies face a wide range of opportunities and challenges when managing data analytics.

Opportunities: When managed properly, data analytics can help a company to understand its customer base better and their preferences. The rapid speed by which a company gathers data can facilitate a real-time response. For example, a company can evaluate customer reviews and feedback and adjust its service and shipping policies accordingly. This specialized knowledge gives companies an advantage over their competitors.

Also, the knowledge gained from data analytics can identify a broader target market and their needs. Such information can create opportunities for new products, services, and revenue streams.

Challenges: If not managed effectively, a company can become quickly overwhelmed by the excessively large volume of data and the quick speed that it accumulates. Companies face other challenges when managing data analytics such as;

- Data collected from multiple locations may have different structures, making it challenging to integrate into one platform. For example, data from websites and spreadsheets accumulates in a column and row format. Information feeding in from e-mails and surveys may have less structure.

- The quality of data is critical for analysis. Companies may not have enough resources to review and clean up data that is accumulated adequately. When data quality is poor, it impacts the effectiveness of data analysis.
- The large volume of data acquired can pose issues if a company does not have adequate storage in place. Lack of room can result in lost or incomplete data and may impact the quality of data analysis.
- Data analysis requires specialized knowledge and skill. A company may not have experienced personnel in place. Without this expertise, incomplete or incorrect assumptions may be made based on the data received.

Why Data and Data Science Capability are Strategic Assets

Data and data science capabilities are strategic assets to an organization as they can improve the effectiveness and efficiency of business processes, aid decision-making, and provide oversight. Both can offer a new perspective about a company's operations, which translates to financial gains.

When companies strategically incorporate data and data science into their business models, they can gain a valuable new perspective about their operations, translating into financial gains and competitive advantage.

Companies that invest in robust data science capabilities can realize several benefits including:

- Identification of new revenue sources and markets
- Gain insight into future trends and reduce uncertainty
- Solve problems and improve decision-making
- Enhance processes by shortening business cycles, improving company oversight, and identifying greater efficiencies
- Understand customer buying habits, helping them to improve their sales and marketing efforts
- Spot risks and weaknesses within a company's operations and take steps to overcome them

Business Intelligence

Business intelligence (BI) combines a variety of tools to enable companies to make better decisions. BI consists of technology-driven processes that rely on methodologies, theories, and applications that transform raw data into useful information that can be used by management to improve organizational performance, identify potential revenue sources, and enter new markets.

Best Practices: BI relies heavily on the quality of data obtained and the management's willingness to use it.

The effectiveness of BI may depend on a company's best practices, such as

- Identify the business need for BI
- Having a written plan of action
- Select sources of data for acquisition
- Obtain buy-in from the user and organization
- Create a data-driven environment

Applications include tools to mine, cleanse, and process data. Software and spreadsheets are typical applications.

Best practices, tools, and applications transform data into useable information for decision-making. Typical outputs, such as dashboards, key performance indicators, and reports are tools that management can use to identify opportunities for improvement in business processes, reduce costs, and to better compete in the marketplace.

Big Data

Big Data refers to the excessively large volume of data that a business collects and the technology used to process it. Big Data includes how a business captures, accumulates, and processes large volumes of information. It is often defined through the four V's;

- Volume – A business accumulates data from a number of locations including website activity, transactions, smart devices, sensors, social media, and other sources. The sheer volume of the information is why it's known as "big data."
- Velocity – The rate at which a business processes data is known as velocity. With extremely large volumes of data coming from multiple locations and in a variety of structures, data must be processed close to real-time in order for it to retain its value.
- Variety – Data comes in multiple formats. It is typically structured in numeric formats and follows a basic set of rules. Information may also come through in an unstructured format such as email messages, videos, text documents, or audio. Unstructured data does not follow specific rules and often requires interpretation.
- Veracity – This concept refers to the quality of the data. With structured and unstructured information coming in at lightning speed, a business needs to effectively cleanse, link, and distribute data across multiple systems. Relationships between data should be properly connected and correlated.

The large volume of data collected by a company can be processed and analyzed to gain more information about its business and customers. Big Data brings a multitude of opportunities to a business including;

- Create an effective strategy – Analysis using large volumes and varieties of data can help a business to understand its customer base, market conditions, and future product or service offerings.
- Operational improvements – The ability to acquire and analyze data quickly allows a company to improve operations and productivity.
- Improve customer service – Greater information obtained from social media, website interactions, and customer relationship management software can help companies to better serve their customers.
- Detect errors – Patterns that emerge from processing large volumes of data can help to identify errors or fraudulent activity. These patterns or anomalies can be identified and acted upon quickly. This is especially helpful for banks and credit card companies to pick out fraudulent activity and notify the customer.

Challenges – Companies face a myriad of challenges when implementing big data strategies including;

- High investment – The ability to process large volumes of data requires may require a significant investment in infrastructure. This includes software, hardware, additional storage capacity, and the appropriate bandwidth to transmit and process large volumes of data.
- Expertise – Companies often need to hire experienced data scientists and analysts to interpret data and address quality issues. Such expertise can be costly.

- Security – Large volumes of data stored by a company can be accessed by breached by unauthorized users or subject to loss due to backup failures.
- Data quality – Data that is pulled from multiple sources needs to be properly cleaned, linked to the appropriate fields, and processed. Inaccuracies or poor format can lead to quality issues that can impact a data's relevance and usefulness.
- Compliance – Privacy concerns have led to increased compliance requirements for companies to follow to ensure that personal information remains secure. They may be required to comply with industry and government standards which can be complex and costly.

Data Mining

Data mining transforms raw data into useful information. It involves combing through volumes of data to identify trends, correlations, and abnormalities. Patterns, connections, and anomalies detected in large sets of data may be used to predict future outcomes.

Data mining is useful for organizations to make better decisions, gain a competitive edge, identify future trends and revenue streams, reduce costs, and provide a deeper understanding of a customer base.

Data mining is influenced by the quality of the data collected, how it is processed, and where it is stored. Mining includes gathering data in a data warehouse. It is stored and managed in the cloud or on a company's internal servers. Data is then accessed and organized. Analytical processes can be applied to the data, allowing for presentation in a format that can be used by management to evaluate the information, such as a spreadsheet, graph, or report.

Data mining techniques include:

- Descriptive modeling – Identifies relationships and groupings in data. It may include such techniques as clustering, affinity grouping, principal component analysis, association rule learning, and anomaly detection.
- Predictive modeling – Uses data to predict future events and trends, such as customer buying habits or credit default. Decision trees, regression analysis, neural networks, and supervised learning models are standard techniques.
- Prescriptive modeling – This technique may be used when data is unstructured. Comment fields, websites, and other text sources typically yield such data. Conventional methods such as if/then analysis and market simulations to optimize ROI are frequently used.

Data mining is the process of locating patterns, collections, and abnormalities in large volumes of data. There are several challenges with data mining such as:

- Volume –The sheer amount of data that is accumulated by organizations can be overwhelming and challenging to navigate. Data gathered from multiple locations may be structured, unstructured, or both, causing integration challenges
- Quality – Data that is missing fields, inconsistent, or requires significant clean-up may be unuseful. Poor data quality may result in data samples that do not adequately reflect the trends, patterns, or correlations in the overall data acquired.
- Conflicting data – When gathered from multiple sources, data that represents the same information, such as names and addresses, may be conflicting.
- Redundancy – Duplication in data acquired impacts the efficiency of processing and analysis. Processing the same information multiple times costs a company time and money.

- Accessibility – Data that is difficult to access or not available can be costly to process. Inaccessibility may require more human resources, complex calculations, and a significant amount of time to extract, process, and analyze.
- Privacy and security concerns – Large volumes of data that may yield sensitive information about customers, financial transactions, or the company itself.
- Updates – Data acquired from multiple platforms may yield inconsistencies as software or collection models may undergo upgrades.
- Cost – Collecting and analyzing large volumes of data can require hardware and software programs that are costly and may be financially-prohibitive for some organizations.

An iterative process is a repetitive function applied in sequential order to generate an output. As data is received and processed, it yields produces information and patterns that are validated and studied, with the results used to refine the iterative process. This process allows for continuous improvement.

- Data mining as a science: As data reflect new information, data mining's iterative process may indicate that a previous step needs refinement. When steps are updated, the results yielded may show patterns in the data. As trends emerge, the data is validated, and the processes refined. The iterative process of data mining is like a science due to its continuous process of validation and refinement.
- Data mining as an art: Effectively mining and interpreting data requires the creativity to see patterns and devise alternative solutions. Data mining touches on art as the process is valued for the ideas that it produces.

Query Tools

Through a query, specific data is obtained from a database. A query is a written command or a set of commands that define the criteria for the requested data to be retrieved. Structured Query Language, or SQL, is a domain-specific language designed to pull data from a relational database. SQL consists of a series of commands used to retrieve data. Commands are structured in a way to direct the tool to extract data based on:

- Location
- Type
- Condition

Commands are used together to narrow down the retrieval to specific data that meets the required criteria or to present it in the desired order, such as smallest to largest. SQL commands can also perform functions such as computing averages and calculating the sum of values.

Insights from Mined Data

Data mining is the process of sorting through large sets of data to identify trends and patterns. Since data may come from multiple locations, such as websites, social media, and email, data mining is typically an automated process. When analysts mine large data sets effectively, they can identify trends and patterns, as well as provide insight into these trends.

Data mining begins when raw data from multiple sources is reformatted into a consistent format. Once cleaned and transformed, large data sets may be mined effectively when an analyst:

- Understands the business purpose – Data acquired from multiple sources is voluminous. Knowing what goals the company is trying to achieve helps an analyst to structure their queries accordingly.

- Asks the right questions – Targeted and direct questions narrow down the scope of data sought. Also, it helps the analyst to determine if the data requested and the results received are useful.
- Exploratory data analysis (EDA) – Extracted data may be analyzed using data visualization and statistical methods. This analysis can identify characteristics of the data, such as patterns, commonalities, or trends. An analyst may also segment that data obtained. Natural ways to group similar data may also target patterns and trends.
- Modeling – Analysts use data modeling to make future predictions based on the data obtained. Modeling may include simulations and machine-learning.
- Validation - Once modeling is complete, an analyst should evaluate the method(s) chosen to determine if it produces the best result for the data set. This evaluation is done by running tests through the model, comparing these results against the actual data for reasonableness.

At this final stage, the data obtained should provide valuable insights into a company's operations and opportunities. Analysts may use forecasting to predict future results, improve business metrics, and increase efficiency.

Analytic Tools

Fitting an Analytic Model to Data

When you take the approach of fitting data to a model, you assume that the model is correct. An analyst would seek data that conforms to the model. However, observed data is fixed, meaning that it doesn't change. Trying to find data that fits the parameter of the model may yield incorrect or inaccurate results.

Conversely, when the analytic model is designed to fit the data, an analyst would start with determining what data or problem they are trying to solve.

Challenges encountered when trying to fit an analytic model to the data include:

- Selecting the optimal model parameters and determining which function(s) will reflect this and return the predicted data set.
- Determining the rate of error based on the fit between the data and the model
- Finding the function that best minimizes the error between the model and the data
- Failing to visual inspect the data for patterns and trends, which may help in the selection of model parameters
- Choosing the right model to use
- Updating the model for parameter changes based on the results found in the data

Types of Data Analytics

Examining data to conclude the information provided is known as data analytics. Four critical types of data analytics evaluate data from different perspectives to assist organizations in their decision-making process;

- Descriptive – This approach focuses on past data to identify what happened. Typically this is done with canned or ad hoc reports. Canned reports may be similar to routine financial statements, KPIs, or other performance metric reports the provide a snapshot of a specific period. An ad hoc report will also reflect past data; however, they are usually not scheduled. Instead, they are generated when more in-depth information is necessary about a specific activity or fluctuation. Descriptive reports designed to tell you "what happened" are often expanded on through other data analytic procedures.

- Diagnostic – Similar to the descriptive approach, diagnostic data analytics are compiled with past data. Diagnostic analytics look at the cause and effect of past data relationships to answer the question of "why" something happened. Under this approach, you may drill-down to the detail or review correlations to gain an understanding as to what caused something to occur or not occur.
- Predictive – Building on the data and results obtained from descriptive and diagnostic procedures, predictive data analytics focuses on what could happen. This approach looks at trends, correlations, and causations found in the data to forecast future outcomes.
- Prescriptive – This is an advanced form of analytics that focuses on what a company should do. It often uses sophisticated analytic tools such as machine learning and algorithms. Prescriptive data analytics uses both internal and external data to test a variety of variables in "what-if" scenarios.

ANALYTIC MODELS

Analytics models such as clustering, classification, and regression, look for similarities and differences in data sets. Classification and regression learning techniques are known as "supervised" when they have defined parameters to examine the data based on past activities. Clustering is an unsupervised learning technique as it looks for natural groupings in the data without any preset conditions.

Clustering – Under this model, similarities of data are seen when the results are grouped, or clustered, together. Clustering is an unsupervised model as there are no set expectations set up to measure the data against. It helps to find structure in data by group and identifies information that is similar and different. By grouping data into smaller datasets, it may be easier to perform further analytics.

Clustering is useful for:

- Large, unstructured data
- An unknown quantity of classes that the data is best divided into
- Finding anomalies in data
- Narrowing down a more extensive data set to a specific category, allowing it to be further evaluated manually

Classification – Labels or other predefined types used to assign values to a particular class. It is considered a supervised approach as the user identifies the labels, or training sets used to categorize the data. These training sets categorize these observations based on previous experience. For example, if a pattern of activity on a network identified as potentially being malicious, the classification will help to determine whether it is a threat or not based on past events. Classification is helpful to use when;

- Labeling customers based on specific factors
- Recommending similar products or services to customers based on their search history
- Predicting one value in a set of values, such as a Yes/No question

Regression – Regression predictive modeling is a statistical method for predicting a continuous variable, such as tomorrow's temperature or sales. This type of analysis evaluates the relationship between two or more variables, known as dependent and independent variables. The dependent variable is the outcome that you are trying to predict. The independent variable impacts the dependent variable. It is also a supervised approach as predefined labels are used. Regression is useful for predicting quantities such as income or price.

Regression

Regression models find the relationship between two or more variables.

Simple regression is defined by the formula: $Y = a + bX$.

The components include:

- Y = the dependent variable
- X = the independent variable
- a = constant or intercept, which means it is the value of Y when X=0
- b = regression coefficient or slope of the line

In this equation, the relationship between the two variables is denoted by a straight line.

The direction of the line indicates the relationship between the two variables.

- When the slope is positive, it shows that there is a positive relationship between the independent and dependent variables. As one variable rises, so will the other.
- Negative slopes reveal an inverse relationship between the independent and dependent variable. When the independent variable increases, the dependent variable will decrease.
- If the corresponding line is parallel to the axis, it reflects that no correlation exists between the independent and dependent variables.

In multiple regression equations, a similar approach is followed except that more than one independent variable exists. A typical formula that describes multiple regression is: $Y = bX_1 + bX_2 + bX_3 + a$

The components include:

- Y = the dependent variable
- X_1 = the first independent variable
- X_2 = the second independent variable
- X_3 = the third independent variable
- a = constant or intercept, which means it is the value of Y when X=0
- b = regression coefficient or slope of the line

Multiple regression equations can have two or more independent variables. Visual representations of multiple regression equations show the results in a two-dimensional plane format.

Coefficient of Determination and the Correlation Coefficient

Both the coefficient of determination and correlation coefficients are statistics that reflect the relationship between two or more variables.

Coefficient of determination (R^2) reflects the proportion of variance that the dependent variable that is predictable from the independent variable. It is often used to predict outcomes by analyzing how the differences in one variable are explained by the variance in another variable.

The coefficient of determination yields a response that ranges between 0.0 and 1.0.

- A result of 1.0 shows a positive relationship (or good fit) between the variables, indicating that the model used has high reliability to predict future outcomes.
- A result of 0.0 indicates that there is no relationship between the variables. The model would not accurately predict future outcomes.
- A result of .30 shows that 30% of the dependent variable is influenced by the independent variable.

Correlation coefficient (R) measures the strength of the relationship between two coefficients. When typical correlation coefficient formulas are applied, they yield results that range between 1 and -1.

- A result of 1 indicates a positive relationship between the two coefficients. For every positive increase in one variable, there is a positive increase in the other variable of a fixed proportion.
- Conversely, a response of -1 reflects a negative relationship. As one variable has a positive increase, the other will reflect a negative decrease of a fixed proportion.
- Should the formula yield a 0, no relationship appears to exist.

TIME SERIES ANALYSES

Time series data refers to a set of data points listed in chronological order. Time series data is presented using line charts.

Time series analysis refers to the methods used to pull meaningful patterns, trends, and statistics from the data. This analysis helps to understand why the data fluctuates. Its results are used for forecasting and simulation. Frequent patterns in time series data include;

- Trends are identifying by long-term increases or decreases in the data presented. In some cases, a pattern may change direction. For example, a new technology product may show an upward rise until an upgraded or faster version replaces it.
- Cyclical trends and patterns reflect fluctuations that don't follow any fixed frequency. Cyclical trends are impacted by outside factors such as economic conditions.
- Seasonal fluctuations are tied to a specific period. It can be a particular time of the year or day of the week. For example, clothing purchases may rise in the summer as parents prepare for children to go back to school.
- Irregular variations have no set patterns or trends in the data. In some cases, they are the variances that remain after removing cyclical or seasonal patterns or trends. They are unpredictable and non-systemic. Highly irregular variations can hide patterns or trends in the data.

REGRESSION ANALYSIS AND TIME SERIES ANALYSIS

Regression analysis is the process of estimating the relationship between a dependent variable and one or more independent variables. Linear regression is the most common form of regression analysis.

The regression analysis has several benefits such as:

- It can help to determine which variables are essential and which are not. For example, consumer use of vitamins may impact the overall health of the population. Yet the quality or contents of the vitamin may not be relevant to its users.

- Results of regression analysis are used to forecast future performance
- Identifying relevant variables and their impact allows for better decisions to be made
- Easier to locate patterns and trends in data

However, regression analysis has drawbacks including:

- Two or more independent variables may have a high correlation to each other, making it difficult to determine which one may be impacting the dependent variable.
- Correlations in data do not necessarily mean that one causes another. As an example, there may be a correlation between smoking cigarettes and alcoholism. However, smoking does not result in alcoholism.

Time series analysis consists of methods to analyze data over a period to understand its characteristics and variations over time.

Benefits of the time series analysis approach include:

- It may help to identify which factor, or factors, impact the fluctuations in data.
- Easy to compare two series of time series data. For example, stock prices could be compared against the unemployment rate to determine if a relationship or pattern exists.
- The results of time series analysis may forecast future performance

The drawbacks to using time series analysis are:

- The analysis may assume that the factor which influenced the series will remain the same over time, which may not be the case
- If a relevant variable is not considered within the analysis, the results may not be indicative of the factors that result in the change
- There may be a time lag when comparing two series of data. For example, crime may rise and fall based on the unemployment rate. However, the unemployment rate may have a natural lag in time when compared to the crime rate.
- It can identify correlation in the data, but not necessarily causation

Standard Error of the Estimate, Goodness of Fit, and Confidence Interval

The standard error of the estimate measures how significant the prediction errors are in a data set. It indicates the level of accuracy of data predictions. A substantial standard of error in the estimate reflects high variability in the data set. The measure of error indicates that there is a lower level accuracy expected in the results. However, a smaller measure of the error of the estimate indicates less variation in the data set. This results in higher expected accuracy in the data results.

The goodness of fit test measures how well your sample data represents the actual population. It looks at the observed data against the results you'd expect from the model. There is a variety of goodness of fit tests with the most popular being the chi-square test.

A **confidence interval** measures the level of certainty in a sampling method. Confidence intervals describe the level of uncertainty associated with a sample estimate of a characteristic of a population, or parameter. Confidence intervals are expressed as a percentage. For example, a 95% confidence interval means that 95% of the sample would include the population parameter.

Predictive Analytic Techniques

Predictive analytics is a series of techniques used to interpret existing data to make informed predictions. There are several models used for predictive analytics, such as;

The **classification model** categorizes data into classes based on historical activity. It is a simple approach that is commonly used to answer "yes or no" questions about the future. It may be used by a retailer to determine if customers who visited their website made a purchase online.

Clustering models group data based on similar characteristics, such as age, buying habits, or location. By examining how the data clusters, a company gains better insights about which attributes that data is clustering around. For example, if a company wants to create a marketing campaign around one of their products, they may use data clustering to determine which age group or zip code is most likely to purchase this based on historical data. The company can then create a targeted marketing campaign to this group

Using a **forecast model**, a company can make data-driven predictions about future activity, based on historical data. A forecast model may be used to predict how many phone inquiries a sales office will receive each week, based on historical activity. Forecast models often consider multiple variables when making predictions. For example, a restaurant owner may use a forecast model to predict the number of customers they expect to receive in the following week. If they have outside seating, they may expand their use to forecast customer levels to consider the impact of rainy or sunny weather.

Looking at **outliers** is a helpful way to pick out trends in data that fall outside of expectations. For example, a spike in consumer complaints may indicate a defective product. Outliers may help to identify fraudulent transactions on a customers' accounts. A spike in high-dollar value electronic purchases for a group of customers who typically use their credit cards for grocery or utility purchases may indicate that fraud has occurred.

A **time series model** collects data points over a period and uses them to identify trends and forecast future activity. This model relies on time as an input parameter. So, a retailer looking to predict how many customers will visit their store may look at the trends from a time series model to make this estimation. Where the model expands its predictive capability is that is can take into account additional variables that can influence the data such as future growth, seasonality, or trends in the marketplace. A time series model can give a retailer a better tool to predict future customer visits.

Exploratory Data Analysis

Exploratory data analysis is often the first step to analyzing data. The analyst applies their judgment toward what the information is telling them. Many times, the data is reflected in a visual format, which makes it easier to pick out patterns. EDA is intended to provide an overall context of the data before choosing a model to solve a problem and interpret findings.

EDA typically uses a univariate or multivariate approach.

- Univariate – Only one variable is analyzed under this approach. This univariate method is helpful to see the data to pick out trends visually. By using a histogram or box plot, the points of data are grouped according to the findings, which can help an analyst see patterns within the data. For example, if a car dealership is trying to determine the most popular color or model of car that is sold, they can visually see these patterns.

- Multivariate – This approach can analyze two or more variables. This type of analysis can reveal relationships and patterns between two or more sets of data.
- Scatter plot – This is a visualization whereby data points are plotted on a graph. One variable is plotted along the X-axis in one color, whereas the other variable is plotted along the Y-axis in another color. The two sets of data points can be analyzed to determine if a relationship or pattern exists between the two. This approach allows for multiple variables to be plotted as identified by their color.
- Bar charts present the variables in a visual format whereby they can be compared against each other

Other approaches that may be used for the univariate or multivariate methods include;

- Map charts, which can be used to pinpoint zip codes or location groupings
- Line charts which may be used to visualize the changes in data over time
- Pie charts which reflect a set of data compared to the whole set

Sensitivity Analysis

When you perform a sensitivity analysis, you are looking at the impact that different independent variables have on a dependent variable. Sensitivity analysis is commonly known as a what-if or simulation analysis whereby you can see how changes in variables may impact the outcome.

A sensitivity analysis lends credibility to financial models as it tests them against many variables. It is used in a variety of business situations. What-if analysis may be used to understand how changes in interest rates or inflation may impact bond prices. As interest rates rise, how will bond prices react? A sensitivity analysis is helpful to see how changes in sales, shares outstanding, or increases in key ratios, such as debt to equity, impact a company's earnings per share. This analysis may help management to determine if they should sell more shares of their stock or the impact that taking on additional debt could have on their share prices.

For example, if you would like to see to understand that impact that increased traffic to your store may have on your sales, you might use a what-if analysis. If a 20% increase in traffic results in a 5% increase in sales, you may run this analysis to see what the impact on your sales would be if your traffic increased 10% or 50%. If customers are price-sensitive, a what-if analysis may help you to understand how pricing and promotions impact sales.

Simulation Models

Simulation models mimic real-world situations. They are often computer programs designed to imitate and test processes and systems. These models allow an organization to change variables and assumptions to see the impact on their current systems without making changes to their operations.

A simulation model allows an organization to test proposed changes in their processes, product lines, or services without impacting their current activities. This can help to assess the risk that they may face, as well as improve the decision-making process.

As an example, if an appliance repair company wants to expand its service offerings, they may use a simulation model to test market demand or to determine if their current infrastructure can support the expansion. Rather than delving into a new market to gain information over time, a simulation model is a low risk means to gather data for decision-making. By making assumptions about future activities, a company can derive estimates based on such things as historical data, trends, or a company's expertise. Dropping assumptions and estimates into a simulation model can help identify risks, such as whether demand is sufficient to offset costs.

There are inherent risks when using an estimate to predict future activity. When a range of estimates can be determined, the Monte Carlo method is used to test the probability of any outcome. By running each estimated value through the model, this method produces many results. In some cases, it may be hundreds, even thousands, depending upon the assumptions and estimates used. These results are often displayed visually and can help management determine the likelihood or probability of an outcome.

A sensitivity analysis, also known as a "what-if" analysis, helps to visually see the impact that a changing independent variable may have on a dependent variable. A construction company may use sensitivity analysis to gain an understanding as to the effect on a project if supplies are delivered late. The study may reveal how a timing delay impacts the overall cost of the project concerning labor, delivery fees, as well as hitting any contractual deadlines.

Benefits to a sensitivity analysis include;

- Lower risk – by analyzing the impact of changing variables, a company can identify risk and come up with solutions before a problem starts. In the case of the construction company, when a shipping delay is imminent, the company may choose to go with a different supplier if the what-if analysis reveals that is would cost less to do so.
- The variables used in the analysis are often vetted and have a reasonable basis for their inclusion.

Drawbacks:

- Independent variables may not always be stand-alone and may be influenced by other factors.
- A what-if analysis requires that you make assumptions about future activities. What happens in the future is difficult to predict, which adds risk to the assumptions and estimates used in the study.

Simulation models replicate a process or event. They are disconnected or separated from the actual process or event and typically run using simulation software. This allows simulation to occur without impacting actual data or operations.

Benefits:

- Simulation models are relatively low risk as they are isolated from active data and operations. A simulation model is a low risk way to test a change to a large-scale operation without impacting its current activities. For example, a company might test the impact that consolidating its manufacturing facilities into one location might have on its production and shipping times.
- Simulation models are highly flexible. They can be used to test one changes in one or more operational processes. It can be used by a variety of industries such as retail, manufacturing, mining, and logistics. Simulation can also be used for training purposes whereby various scenarios are introduced to teach employees how to react.
- Simulation models can be used to test one specific process or an entire business operation from ordering, fulfillment, to shipping. It can handle large-scale operations and complex calculations.

- It allows you to study changing variables and their impact on the outcome. For example, you can test the impact that bad weather or political unrest could have on your supply chain or sales.

Drawbacks:

- Without having a standardized approach to follow, creating a simulation model can be a challenge when you don't have a reference or guide to follow.
- Building a simulation model can be expensive and take months, even years, to create.
- The data used in a simulation model must be validated. This can be an extensive process whereby you would need to test simulated data against actual data to see how closely the simulation model recreates what occurred.

What-If (Goal-Seeking) Analysis

With goal-seeking analysis, you are essentially working backwards as there is a set or determined output. It is the input variable that is tested to reach the desired output. Goal seeking works with only one input variable.

It is a form of a what-if analysis whereby the calculation based on changing input values to see how they impact the desired output. This type of analysis allows you to test a range of scenarios to see their possible outcome.

For example, if a company is looking to generate $100,000 in sales, the input variable is the unknown that the company is attempting to solve. If the selling price of the company's product is $50, they would need to sell 2,000 units to reach their $100,000 goal.

Limitations of Data Analytics

Analyzing large volumes of raw data to identify correlations, trends, and answer questions is known as data analytics. Data collection and processing is typically automated. Such analysis can provide valuable insights into customer buying habits, future trends, or efficiency improvements.

However, data analytics does present limitations.

- Large volumes of data that are pulled in from multiple sources may have inconsistencies in their quality and format. This can pose a challenge when analyzing data and identifying trends.
- The correlations and links found within the data may not be meaningful or related. For example, you may see a rise in the birth rate as well as a rise in the sale of butter. While both appear to be trending upwards, there may be little if any correlation between the two. However, if there is a rise in the employment rate, there could be a meaningful correlation with the rise in butter sales as more people are working and can afford it.
- Data analytics can take you down the wrong path. You may detect a relationship or trend in the data, but if it's not related to the question that you are trying to answer – it can take you down the wrong path.
- Large volumes of data may be difficult to access, transfer, or use in multiple analysis easily. This can slow down the data analytics process.
- With companies collecting and storing large volumes of data, they may be more susceptible to security breaches.

Data Visualization

Data visualization is a graphical representation of information. Best practices to avoid the distortion the data include:

- Have a clear purpose - Define what purpose the data gathered and presented will serve. A clear purpose can prevent the presentation of irrelevant information.
- Use the right format - The presented data's relationship drives the presentation chosen for table and graph designs.
    - Bar graphs are used to show the differences between groups of data.
    - Pie charts compare parts, or percentages, of a whole
    - Line charts are used to compare values over a period.
    - Scatter plots are used to plot data for two variables of data. A scatter plot allows you to see naturally groupings of data.

  When the wrong presentation is used, data can be distorted and not reflect results.
- Organize your data in a readable format - Data presentation should have a natural flow that makes sense to a reader if you are reporting on data over time, considering presenting this by year or month. When using colors to present data, use contrasting colors helps data to stand out. Similar hues, on the other hand, can be confusing. However, if too many colors are used to present the data, it can overshadow the table's results or graph.
- Present data in a meaningful way - When data is presented in a format using an X and Y axis, use the proper "0" baseline. If the X or Y axis does not start with "0", this presentation is often referred to as a truncated graph and misleading.

Data Visualization Options

There are a variety of options and presentation approaches used for data visualization. The most used are listed below.

- A boxplot, also known as box and whisker plot, shows the range of data from its minimum, 1st quartile, 2nd quartile (or median), 3rd quartile, and maximum. The data groups presented typically have a relationship with each other. The boxplot will show the average or median of each group, plus the minimum and maximum outliers. This is an excellent format to use when you have a large amount of data and need to compare two or more sets.
- Scatter plots show the relationship between two variables, marked as a data point on the graph. There are multiple data points in a scatter plot, which helps to show the natural groupings of data and outliers.
- Dot plots visually present the frequency of data. They show one variable of data across the X-axis, using one dot for each data point. For example, if you were plotting the number of siblings each child has in a class of 10 children, your X-axis may range from 0 siblings to 4 siblings. There would be a dot in each category in a linear fashion.
- Tables are a means to present multiple data points and graphical representations, such as icons and sparklines, in one place. Data is organized into rows and columns, making its presentation easy for reporting. While they are a helpful way to present various data, it's best to limit the amount of information shown on a table to keep the reader from being overwhelmed.
- Histograms visualize data over a period. They are vertical bar charts that show how the data is distributed. Histograms are an easy way to see if most values fall within a scale of measurement and how much variation there may be.
- Dashboards are a graphic representation of key data points and metrics. Dashboards give the user a snapshot of the health of business, department, or program.

- Bar Charts are a graphic representation of different sets of data using a rectangular bar format. They are suitable for comparing data between other groups or to look at changes over time. For example, an appliance store may use a bar chart to show how many refrigerators, stoves, or dishwashers they sold in a month. It may be used to see how many refrigerators were sold each month over one year.
- Pie Charts are visual representations used to compare the parts of a whole. For example, they may show the age breakdown of a school's population. A pie chart may reflect relative values, such as the number of kindergarteners attending Elementary School A compared with the number of kindergarteners attending Elementary School B.
- Line Charts show data points over a continuous variable such as time or money. A single line is drawn to connect the variables for each set of data. Multiple sets of data can be presented on a line chart, in which each group has its variables connected. Line charts are useful for identifying trends and fluctuations.
- Bubble Charts are like scatter plots as they are the visual representation of two variables. Rather than using a dot, as you'd expect to see on a scatter plot, they use a bubble whose size is relative to a third variable.

Data visualization presents information in a chart, graph, or another format to show a visual picture of the data.

There are several benefits to using visualization techniques when presenting data.

- Better understanding – Data visualization helps the user understand the data presented and its relevant relationships. Data visualization can be especially helpful when comparing two or more sets of data.
-
- Easier to process – When a visual picture of data is presented, it is often easier for people to understand. This may be the case if the information is complicated or difficult to understand.
- Meaningful – Not only is the data presented important, but the visual tool used can make it more meaningful to an audience. Presenting data by geographical location using a bar chart may be helpful; however, using a heat map format can show the magnitude of the data by the intensity of its color.
- Benchmarks – A visual representation of data is helpful when measuring results against benchmarks

While data visualization has many benefits, it's not without its disadvantages. These limitations include;

- Oversimplification – Data visualization is intended to present large volumes of information in an easier format. Oversimplified visuals, however, may not convey the underlying message of the data.
- The human element – Data is subject to interpretation and may only include the assumptions that the analyst determines are important. This bias may skew the results of the data presented.

- Poor design – Choosing the wrong visualization tool may report results that are confusing or difficult to interpret. For example, a pie chart is used to visually present the breakdown of one set of data, such as the number of children that make up each grade in an elementary school. If you were to compare the same information for two schools, putting this on one pie chart would be confusing. A poor design also refers to the presentation. Data presented in a graph that uses an X and Y axis should start with a "0" baseline. If the baseline starts with a different number, the results will be skewed in the presentation.
- The in-depth analysis may be limited – Data visualization presents a summary view without the detail. Without the underlying data, any in-depth research necessary will be limited.

CMA Practice Test

Multiple Choice

1. How does a budget containing inaccurate data impact an organization's future performance?

a. The organization can forecast the effect of economic changes
b. The organization is unable to obtain financing and capital needs
c. The organization is unable to properly plan and set attainable goals
d. The organization can make adjustments the following year

2. Which information is needed to develop an effective budget?

a. Historical financial data, projected expenses, and anticipated revenues
b. Historical financial data only
c. Historical expenses and revenues
d. Projected expenses and anticipated revenues

3. Which budgeting method does not use performance data from prior years as the basis for budget figures?

a. Authoritative budgeting
b. Zero-based budgeting
c. Capital budgeting
d. Participative budgeting

4. What type of information is used when performing a regression analysis?

a. Production schedules
b. Projected sales or revenues
c. Return on investment
d. Interest rates

5. A learning curve...

a. shows the efficiencies gained from experience
b. uses historical data as a basis for forecasting
c. uses statistical techniques for forecasting
d. determines inefficiencies in the production process

6. Which forecasting technique gives more weight to newer data and less weight to older data?

a. Time series analysis
b. Exponential smoothing
c. Multiple regression analysis
d. Payback technique

7. Organizations use Kaizen budgeting to...

a. allocate funds and resources to projects
b. determine how the budget will attain the organization's goals
c. continually improve the budgeting process
d. allocate funds and resources based on activity or process

8. A master budget's purpose is to...

a. control the day to day operations of the organization
b. determine the goals of the organization for a 10 year period
c. allocate resources for capital expansion
d. allow for changes in the budget based on performance

9. What is the major difference between a static budget and a flexible budget?

a. The budget period used to forecast production results
b. The types of revenues and costs associated with the projected production
c. The ability to modify budget figures based on actual production
d. The number of production levels that are used in the forecast

10. Which of the following is NOT considered part of the production budget?

a. Manufacturing costs
b. Distribution costs
c. Inventory levels
d. Supervisor salaries

11. A contribution margin is the difference between...

a. the total revenues of the organization and the total revenues of a product
b. the total costs of the organization and the total costs of a product
c. the total revenues and the total fixed costs of a product
d. the total revenues and the total variable costs of a product

12. Which item is contained in the financing section of a cash budget?

a. Accounts receivables expected to be collected from customers
b. Cash receipts expected to be received during the budget period
c. Loan amounts expected to be repaid during the budget period
d. Cash balances to be maintained during the budget period

13. The main reason for building a pro forma financial statement is to...

a. assist in a corporation's annual audit
b. predict and plan for future operations and financing needs
c. anticipate cash flow needs
d. none of the above

14. What is the first step taken to develop a pro forma cash flow statement?

a. Determining the amount of cash the organization has on hand
b. Listing sources of cash income
c. Identifying potential sources of working capital
d. Computing profitability ratio

15. Which type of pro forma financial statement is used to predict how an organization would utilize assets in the future?

a. Pro forma income statement
b. Pro forma statement of financial position
c. Projected balance sheet
d. Pro forma cash flow statement

16. Which statistical method is used to determine progress an organization has made toward meeting its goals and objectives?

a. Product profitability analysis
b. Process costing
c. Performance measurement
d. Benchmarking

17. Which term describes a unit within an organization that generates income separately from the other units?

a. Revenue center
b. Cost center
c. Profit center
d. Investment center

18. The difference between budget amounts and actual amounts is called...

a. cost variance
b. budget variance
c. profitability variance
d. revenue variance

19. Management by exception involves the analysis of activities...

a. by executive management
b. that are mutually exclusive of other activities
c. that operate at a loss
d. that differ from planned results

20. Which concept underscores the importance of accounting performance measurement in the decision making process?

a. Supply chain management
b. Responsibility accounting
c. Generally Accepted Accounting Principles
d. Total Quality Management

21. Contribution margins are used to...

a. define market segments for a product
b. allocate costs to a product
c. set a price for a product
d. determine the break-even point of a product

22. Which method is NOT used in transfer pricing?

a. Negotiated transfer pricing method
b. Market-based pricing method
c. Fixed cost-based pricing method
d. Variable pricing method

23. The purpose of using standards for performance evaluation and measurement is to...

a. measure efficiency and costs
b. determine the profitability of an investment
c. measure earnings from an increase in sales
d. assess a value to the organization's book value

24. What is the price-earnings ratio?

a. The amount of earnings derived from one dollar's worth of stock
b. The share price of a company's stock compared to its earnings per share
c. The price at which one share of stock sells in a financial market
d. The operating income that an investment earns

25. Which statement is true when contrasting the differences between return on investment and residual income?

a. Residual income measures a rate of return
b. Return on investment earns a lower return on investment
c. Return on investment considers all investment opportunities
d. Residual income measures performance above an expected amount

26. Using the balanced scorecard concept in performance management helps an organization achieve which goal?

a. Provide feedback on how goals are being met
b. Manage the performance of a strategic plan
c. Ensure continuous quality improvement
d. Minimize production delays and backlogs

27. Which business process measure is a component of the balanced scorecard concept?

a. Ability to retain customers
b. Ability to meet customer demands
c. Training employees in new processes
d. Ability to respond to customer needs

28. Controllability is used to administer organizational planning activities by...

a. preparing an annual budget
b. managing sales
c. managing tasks and jobs, costs, and revenues
d. creating pro forma income statements

29. Which type of expense is NOT included in the cost of goods sold?

a. Labor expenses
b. Material expenses
c. Overhead expenses
d. Sales expenses

30. Which is true with respect to the difference that variable costing versus absorption costing would have on an income statement?

a. Absorption costing uses variable costs classified by job
b. Inventory figures are reported differently
c. Variable costing defers fixed overhead costs
d. Costs are not reported as a cost of goods sold

31. What is the difference between job order costing and process costing?

a. Process costing allocates costs over a product's life cycle
b. Job order costing allocates costs to a production department
c. Job order costing allocates costs to a job, contract, or order
d. Process costing allocates costs to a product

32. Which type of costing method is used in just-in-time manufacturing environments?

a. Job order costing
b. Process costing
c. Backflush costing
d. Operation costing

33. Which item is considered an explicit cost?

a. Utilities
b. Goodwill
c. Cost of goods sold
d. Office supplies

34. The purpose of using a cost allocation method is to...

a. control costs and use resources more efficiently
b. provide for continuous quality improvement
c. determine the sales price of a product
d. set production capacities

35. Which is not a characteristic of just-in-time manufacturing?

a. Reduction of production time
b. Creation of a production plan
c. Decrease of manufacturing time
d. Increase of workflow efficiency within the marketplace

36. The least capable resource in a drum-buffer-rope system is the...

a. buffer
b. throughput
c. rope
d. capacity constraint resource

37. Which is a competitive advantage gained by using value chain analysis?

a. Obtaining materials at a low cost and high quality
b. Designing time-savings tasks and procedures
c. Improving operations by comparing performance to other organizations
d. Providing more efficient work processes

38. Which action is necessary to implement a total quality management system?

a. Collecting qualitative and quantitative data
b. Setting a budget and schedule for the program
c. Creating control charts
d. Developing cause and effect diagrams

39. Which continuous improvement method emphasizes efficiency and productivity in the workforce?

a. Pareto principle
b. Generic benchmarking
c. Best practice analysis
d. Kaizen

40. Which benefit is NOT a direct result of benchmarking?

a. Improvement of operations
b. Creation manufacturing efficiency
c. Increase of customer base
d. Measurement of ability to compete

41. Which is NOT a component of internal control?

a. Control environment
b. Risk assessment
c. Organizational structure
d. Information

42. Which legislation prohibits the use of bribery to create business relationships?

a. Foreign Corrupt Practices Act of 1977
b. Sarbanes-Oxley Act of 2002
c. Securities Exchange Act of 1933
d. Pendleton Act of 1883

43. Which service is provided by an internal auditor?

a. Determining compliance with laws and regulations
b. Improving procurement practices
c. Investigating embezzlement claims
d. Collecting past due accounts receivables

44. What method compares actual performance with potential performance?

a. Operational audit
b. Compliance audit
c. Gap analysis
d. Quality Audit

45. Which step is NOT used to maintain control over information systems?

a. Identify risks to achieving accurate financial reports
b. Properly train employees
c. Develop written policies
d. Use external auditors to determine proper monitoring procedures

46. Processing controls are used to help maintain...

a. security of data
b. correct performance of applications
c. proper display of data
d. regular backups of data

47. Which critical task should be first consideration when building an effective disaster recovery plan?

a. Data encryption
b. Identification of authorized users
c. Assignment of recovery tasks to key employees
d. Identification of vulnerabilities

48. Which is the stated purpose of the Institute of Management Accountants Statement of Ethical Professional Practice?

a. Providing for the accurate accounting of financial data
b. Limiting the scope of an auditor's responsibility during an audit
c. Outlining disciplinary actions for accountants
d. Setting standards of competence, confidentiality, integrity, and credibility

49. What are the competency standards of the Institute of Management Accountants?

a. Keeping information confidential
b. Continuing education, compliance with laws, decision support information and good judgment
c. Avoiding conflicts of interest, maintain ethical behavior
d. Fair and objective information, full disclosure

50. According to the Institute of Management Accountants, a management accountant demonstrates credibility by...

a. providing fair and objective information
b. informing subordinates to keep information confidential
c. performing activities responsibly
d. avoiding conflicts of interest

Essay Questions

Scenario for questions 1-4

A Swiss army knife producer, the Zurich Corporation, has used the following standard costs for its steel materials, labor, and manufacturing overhead:

	Standard quantity	Standard rate	Standard cost
Direct material	200 g	$19/kg	$3.80
Direct labor	1 hr	$12/hr	$12.00
Variable overhead	1.1 hrs	$5/hr	$5.50

The actual costs for the Zurich Corporation in the previous month were as follows. The company employs 300 laborers who worked an average of 165 hours over the previous month, with an average wage of $11.00/hour. Zurich Corp. had 400 kg of steel inventory at month-beginning, purchased 10,000 kg of steel for $205,000, and had 250 kg remaining as unused inventory at month-end. The variable manufacturing overhead costs for the business are assigned on the basis of direct labor hours, and these costs for the month totaled $255,000. With all these costs, the Zurich Corp. produced 49,000 knives.

Question 1

1. Determine the price, quantity, and total variances for Zurich Corp's direct materials costs.
2. What are some possible causes for these variances?
3. What recommendations would you make to the Zurich Corp. leadership for improving direct materials efficiency?

Question 2

1. Determine the rate, efficiency, and total variances for Zurich Corp's direct labor costs.
2. What are some possible causes for these variances?
3. What recommendations would you make to the Zurich Corp. leadership for improving direct labor efficiency?

Question 3

1. Determine the spending, efficiency, and total variances for Zurich Corp's variable overhead costs.
2. What are some possible causes for these variances?
3. What recommendations would you make to the Zurich Corp. leadership for addressing their overall variance issues?

Question 4

List other variance analyses the company could do to test its efficiency, and explain how such analyses would be of assistance.

Scenario for questions 5-8

Smith Equipment Co. manufactures bulldozers to be sold to companies in the construction and mining industries. Smith manufactures two kinds of bulldozers, the Plus and the Deluxe. The Plus has a selling price of $90,000, the Deluxe $110,000. In the most recent quarter Smith manufactured 20 Plus bulldozers and 10 Deluxe bulldozers and sold 12 Plus bulldozers and 8 Deluxe bulldozers.

The production of the Plus bulldozers was specifically ramped up in the most recent quarter in anticipation of increased sales for the following quarter. In this quarter, the general, selling, and administrative expenses totaled $250,000, while fixed overhead costs totaled $120,000.

The variable product costs for the two bulldozers are as such:

	Plus	Deluxe
Direct material per unit	$30,000	$42,000
Direct labor per unit	$13,000	$15,000
Variable overhead per unit	$6,000	$6,000

Question 5

Compute the different reported incomes if Smith Equipment Co. were to use variable costing and if it were to use absorption costing in assigning costs to its products.

Question 6

What would be some advantages and disadvantages to Smith Equipment Co. of using variable costing over absorption costing?

Question 7

Would you recommend process costing or job-order costing to Smith Equipment Co.? Why?

Question 8

The leadership of the business realizes the need for new capital given their business activities and investments and expected timeline for future profits. Accordingly, the leadership approaches you to prepare financial information to be given to a bank in seeking approval of a loan. What kind of financial information should you prepare, and how would you go about doing so?

Answer Key and Explanations

1. C: The organization is unable to properly plan and set attainable goals. Because budgets play a key role in planning business operations, communicating organizational goals, organizing jobs and processes, and maintaining control, inaccurate budget data can have far-reaching adverse effects throughout the organization. Budgets help determine where to deploy resources needs, when new financing or capital expenditures are needed, and how to effectively manage inventory. Organizations use budgets to estimate earnings and spending during a specified period of time. Future budgets are based on previous financial records and are adjusted to reflect business and economic changes. Inaccurate data can cause inaccurate planning.

2. A: Historical financial data, projected expenses, and anticipated revenues. An effective budget starts with historical financial data at its base. It's important to have accurate historical data and sound projected data so that benchmark figures can be used to evaluate success or failure. Projected expenses and anticipated revenues are used to adjust historical data to create a realistic budget that will meet the goals and objectives of the organization. Because budgets outline the expected income and costs, they communicate expected operational results. Companies use this as a blueprint to then assign accountability for tasks and identify the means by which goals would be achieved.

3. B: Zero-based budgeting. Zero-based budgeting disregards historical data and focuses only on data needed to produce future results. For each budget period, figures are determined based on the organization's goals. Zero-based budgeting has proven effective as a tool for reducing budgetary slack, when implemented periodically, such as one out of every three or four years of the budget cycle. It is not necessary to use zero-based budgeting every year to reduce the occurrence of budgetary slack.

4. D: Interest rates. Regression analysis is a statistical method that measures the relationship between a dependent variable and a series of changing, or independent, variables. It would be helpful in determining how changing variables, such as interest rates and taxes, would affect the price of a variable like a financial investment. By measuring the historical changes of the independent variables in relation to the dependent variable, the future value of the dependent variable can be predicted. It has also been useful in predicting trends.

5. A: Shows the efficiencies gained from experience. A learning curve is a graphical depiction of the efficiencies gained from experience. It shows the relationship between the number of units produced and the time spent per unit. Learning curve analysis is used to make pricing decisions, schedule labor and production resources, develop capital budgets, and set wage rates. The theory is that cost per unit of output will decrease as learning and experience are gained. An individual learning a task will gradually become more efficient and less hesitant, thereby making fewer mistakes, learning to automate, and adjusting performance.

6. B: Exponential smoothing. Exponential smoothing uses a weighted moving average of historical data as the forecasting basis, giving more weight to recent data and less weight to older data. New data is given more weight because the future is more likely to resemble the recent past rather than the distant past. Exponential smoothing is used for short-term forecasting for financial market and economic data. To calculate exponential smoothing, a new forecast is the sum of the old forecast plus a percentage of the difference between the old forecast and the actual data for that same time period.

7. C: Continually improve the budgeting process. In Kaizen, each aspect of the budgeting process is evaluated to implement improvements to be incorporated into the next budgeting cycle. It favors small changes on a regular basis, rather than infrequent but sweeping changes. Kaizen is the Japanese term for "continuous improvement." Project budgeting allocates money and resources to individual projects such as the construction of facilities, acquisition of land, or purchase of equipment. Zero-based budgeting requires budgeted figures to be justified for each new budget period, and show how the budget will attain the goals of the organization. Activity-based budgeting, based on activities and business processes, forecasts labor and financial resources needed to achieve an organization's goals.

8. A: Control the day to day operations of the organization. The master budget is also known as the annual budget: It's the compilation of the budgets of each individual department, and consists of sales, production and cash budgets, and forecasted balance sheet. The annual budget outlines the organization's plans for its fiscal year and controls the day to day operations, setting priorities for accomplishing the long-term goals of the organization by allocating resources to each of the activities outlined in the organization's strategic plan.

9. D: The number of production levels that are used in the forecast. Static budgets forecast one level of production results for a given budget period, and the associated costs. Flexible budgets project revenues and costs for several production levels. Static budgets often differ from actual results, since assumptions about input and output values are made prior to the start of the budget period and are not changed. A flexible budget is based on actual output, and when compared with the static budget, variances become apparent. Flexible budgeting allows for change during the budget period; management can see variances between budget and actual results and take action to improve performance. Flexible budgets compare actual costs with projected costs for the actual production level in order to provide greater control over costs.

10. B: Distribution costs. Distribution costs are a part of the selling and administrative budget. The production budget is an estimate of the amount of product an organization will need to produce during the budget period. The production budget consists of overhead costs that are directly related to manufacturing, and includes forecasts for material, labor, manufacturing supplies, supervisor salaries, factory maintenance, equipment repair, and utilities. Management uses the sales budget and forecasted inventory levels to determine the production budget.

11. D: The total revenues and the total variable costs of a product. The contribution margin is the difference between the total revenues received from a product, and the total variable costs incurred by that product. The money represented by the margin can be used for fixed costs and to produce profits. The contribution margin also helps determine if a product can be sold below the normal sales price when manufacturing capacity is not being fully utilized, and is a useful indicator for evaluation of management and employee performance.

12. C: Loan amounts expected to be repaid during the budget period. The cash budget is determined by taking the cash available at the beginning of the budget period, adding sources of cash, and subtracting cash disbursements (such as loan payments). This helps determine a company's need for financing to meet cash flow needs. The cash budget contains four sections—receipts, disbursements, cash surplus or deficit, and financing:

- Receipts— contains beginning cash balance, expected accounts receivables collected and anticipated cash receipts
- Disbursements— projected cash payments.

- Cash surplus or deficit— difference between cash receipts and disbursements
- Financing— expected new loans and repayment amounts

13. B: Predict and plan for future operations and financing needs. Pro forma financial statements are financial forecasts based on past operations, organizational goals, and anticipated future events. By emphasizing current or projected results, pro formas help companies determine deployment of assets and funds, and predict income and spending. Pro forma income statements are used to predict sales and expenses. Pro forma statements of financial position show the assets that will be used by accounts receivable, inventory, and equipment. Pro forma cash flow statements are used to determine the possibility of cash shortages. Pro formas are commonly used to show the future effects of a potential merger or acquisition, a new capital structure or infusion of funds.

14. A: Determining the amount of cash the organization has on hand. The present cash position is the starting point for a pro forma cash flow statement. Sources of cash income include accounts receivables from prior period's sales, and sales made and paid for during the current period. Then, all sources of future cash inflows and all uses of future cash must be compiled, including cost of goods sold, operating expenses, and income taxes. The cash uses are subtracted from the cash sources to determine the net change in cash position. Finally, the net change in cash position is added to the starting cash figure to arrive at the starting cash figure for the particular pro forma cash flow period.

15. B: Pro forma statement of financial position. The pro forma statement of financial position is a projected balance sheet. It's used to determine how, and how much of the, assets will be utilized in the future— accounts receivable, inventory, and equipment. In a pro forma statement of financial position, each item on the balance sheet must be projected for the budget period.

16. C: Performance measurement. Performance measurement indicates how effectively and efficiently an organization conducts business, using statistics to measure progress in meeting stated goals and objectives. Ideally, improvements to various components of a business' operations would result from a review of performance measurement. The performance evaluation measures used include revenue center, cost center, profit center, and investment center. The performance measurement process should involve process improvement, employee participation, reporting requirements, future planning, total organization improvement, realistic goals, and management commitment.

17. C: Profit center. A profit center is a distinct unit within an organization that adds directly to bottom line profit. It can be a product line, a geographic area, a single retail outlet, manufacturing unit, or department/division. A revenue center generates revenues, and is usually considered profit centers because it is assumed that the revenue center will earn more income than the costs it incurs. A cost center has no control over income and does not generate any. Examples of cost centers include data entry, records retention, human resources, assembly, and production departments. An investment center, usually upper management or the corporate offices, controls costs, revenues, and investments.

18. B: Budget variance. Budget variances are the differences between budget amounts and actual amounts, calculated by subtracting the standard (or budgeted) costs from the actual costs, then multiplying the remainder by the standard units of activity. Variance analysis attempts to find a cause for these differences and examines the effects a variance can have on an organization. Budget variances can be analyzed using two different methods—the two-way analysis and the three-way analysis.

19. D: That differs from planned results. Management by exception is a management control technique that analyzes activities where actual results are significantly lower than planned results. The causes of the deviation are investigated using decision support systems, expert systems, and performance reporting. Once determined, management reviews and implements courses of action intended to correct the causes.

20. B: Responsibility accounting. Responsibility accounting is an overall concept that involves the processes of collection, summary, and reporting of financial information for responsibility centers. Responsibility centers can encompass an organization's cost centers, profit centers, revenue centers, and investment centers. Managers of responsibility centers are accountable for their decisions concerning costs, revenues, and profits, and for taking action with respect to variances between actual and expected results. Responsibility accounting, therefore, is a key underlying concept in a decision making process that tracks costs, revenues, and profits for each responsibility center. In responsibility accounting, management's performance is evaluated based on how well costs, revenues, and profits meet expected results.

21. D: Determine the break-even point of a product. Contribution margins determine how much of each unit sold is used to cover fixed costs, therefore, an important part of cost-volume-profit analysis and break-even analysis. Contribution margins are calculated by subtracting unit variable cost from unit revenue. A company's market segments are determined from its strategic business units to implement individual strategic planning for the products and customers served. Cost allocation associates costs with cost objectives by tracking and accumulating costs tied to a specific object, then selecting a method that identifies the cost with the object. Transfer pricing is used to set prices for services, evaluate financial performance, and determine the contribution a profit center makes toward net income.

22. C: Fixed cost-based pricing method. Transfer pricing is used when a product or service is sold internally between an organization's divisions or departments. The five pricing methods used are:

- Market-based price— actual amount paid
- Cost-based price— marginal cost of funds
- Full cost price— markup covering fixed costs added to manufacturing cost
- Variable cost price— various price points depending on customer or time period
- Negotiated transfer price— set by agreement between buyer and seller

23. A: Measure efficiency and costs. Standards are used in performance evaluation to measure efficiency and costs, keeping tasks within an allowable time frame with consideration to the task's scope. They're set for the expected output for each employee or process, the time required to accomplish a task or complete a process, and the allowable and acceptable levels for mistakes, waste, and spoilage. Return on investment is used to measure the amount of money or profit that is gained on an investment. Earnings quality refers to how earnings are made, and considers whether an increase in sales or a decrease in costs is responsible. The book to market ratio is a valuation method that compares an organization's book value to its market value.

24. B: The share price of a company's stock compared to its earnings per share. The price-earnings ratio values the market share price of a company's stock compared to its earnings per share. It is calculated by dividing market value per share by earnings per share. The price-earnings ratio shows how much an investor pays for a share of stock for each dollar of earnings. Earnings yield is the amount of earnings derived from each dollar of stock, calculated by dividing the earnings per share by the market price for each share of stock. Market value is the price at which a share of stock sells in a financial market, based on what investors are willing to pay. Residual income is the amount of operating income that an investment earns above a minimum level of return on assets.

25. D: Residual income measures performance above an expected amount. Residual income measures an amount of income in dollars while return on investment measures a rate of return. Residual income is used to evaluate performance based on an excess of income over the expected income, with the company's objective being to attain the highest level possible. The objective of return on investment is to attain the highest return on investment percentage. Residual income is preferred over return on investment as a performance measurement because it promotes investment opportunities with a higher rate of return than the cost of invested capital. When return on investment is used as a performance measurement, investment opportunities that lower the rate of return will not be undertaken, even if the investment would be beneficial to the organization.

26. C: Ensure continuous quality improvement. The balanced scorecard approach is a non-financial measure of performance evaluation, with the goal of continuous quality improvement. The balanced scorecard approach uses several performance measurements to determine how well the organization is meeting its objectives. These performance measurements are linked to financial outcomes, customer outcomes, and business process outcomes.

27. B: Ability to meet customer demands. Business process measures are internal processes—either mission-oriented or support in nature— that work to indicate how well a business is operating. Mission-oriented processes include the ability to keep up with technology and creating a more efficient manufacturing environment. Support processes may include the introduction of new products and ability to meet customer demands for a product. The learning and growth measures include employee training, employee self-improvement, and organizational self-improvement. The customer measures focus on the customers' needs and satisfaction with the business' products and services.

28. C: Managing tasks and jobs, costs, and revenues. Controllability is a manager's ability to influence those individuals that perform tasks, incur costs and generate revenues. The controllability efforts of managers include monitoring costs, and determining where and how costs can be reduced. Costs are controlled, in part, by a manager's decisions regarding personnel and workflow, and the procedures used to ensure jobs and tasks are completed in a timely and efficient manner. In making these decisions, managers rely on the annual budget as the foundation of the cost control process. The actual costs for the budget period are compared to the annual budget and the evaluation process helps set new plans to reduce costs and increase revenues.

29. D: Sales expenses. The cost of goods sold is the sum of costs incurred in the production of products, including direct material expenses, direct labor expenses, and overhead expenses. These expenses can be either fixed or variable. Overhead cost is the sum of all manufacturing costs except direct materials and direct labor. Overhead cost includes indirect material costs, indirect labor costs, depreciation, equipment setup costs, quality control costs, maintenance costs, employee benefit costs, payroll taxes, and insurance costs.

30. B: Inventory figures are reported differently, variable costing and absorption costing report inventory figures differently. In variable costing, variable manufacturing costs are included in the inventory figure. In absorption costing, fixed and variable manufacturing costs are included in the inventory figure. When absorption costing is used, the data provided cannot be used for cost-volume-profit analysis because there is no distinction between fixed and variable costs. Variable costing, on the other hand, uses only variable costs which are classified by job or task. When using absorption costing, fixed overhead costs incurred in the current period are deferred to future reporting periods when inventory levels increase. When these inventory items are sold, the fixed overhead costs are reported as a cost of goods sold.

31. C: Job order costing allocates costs to a job, contract, or order. Job order costing distributes costs to a respective job, contract, or order. It identifies direct costs with a specified unit of production or service. Job order costing is used when an organization performs custom manufacturing jobs in which costs need to be applied to a specific customer's order. Process costing distributes costs to the respective department or production process. Direct materials, direct labor, and overhead are charged to the department or process that uses the cost. Activity-based costing distributes expenses among a range of an organization's products depending on the actions performed within the organization. Each employee's time is allocated between the activities that are performed. Life-cycle costing keeps track of the income and expenses of a product during its entire life cycle, extending from the research and development phases through the introduction, growth and maturity stages and to the decline stage.

32. C: Backflush costing. Just-in-time manufacturing environments use backflush costing because the costing process is not performed, nor are costs calculated, until the products are finished. Once completed, the costs are finalized and assigned throughout the system to each product. Operation costing, a cross between job order costing and process costing, is used by organizations that produce a number of similar products with each individual product a slight variation of the basic design. The types of activities that are best suited for job order costing include construction, accounting and legal services, printing and publishing, automobile and equipment maintenance, and consulting. Process costing is most effective in industries that produce only a few products, such as food products, textiles, chemicals and utilities.

33. D: Office supplies. Explicit costs are tangible business expenses that include wages, office rent, office supplies, costs of goods sold, and legal fees. Fixed costs are costs of doing business that do not fluctuate depending on the level of production or the time period. Examples of fixed costs are rents, insurance, salaried payroll, and utility bills. An implicit cost is an opportunity cost incurred when a business uses its own resources to finance one project over another. Variable costs are those costs that change, depending on the activities in which the business is involved or with the level of production. Variable costs are considered to be a part of cost of goods sold, such as inventory costs for a retailer and material costs for a manufacturer

34. A: Control costs and use resources more efficiently. Cost allocation is the process of describing costs according to the period in which they are incurred, the process in which they are used, or the department that incurs the cost. After the cost has been incurred and classified, it must be assigned to a product. When costs are reported in this manner, they can be controlled more easily and resources are used more efficiently. Cost allocation methods are useful in the decision making process since they provide an income measurement usable both inside the organization and by external parties, such as investors. Cost allocation methods can be used to determine the price at which a product should be sold.

35. B: Creation of a production plan. As the name indicates, just-in-time manufacturers purchase and receive materials just before they're needed to build a product. Just-in-time manufacturing helps producers identify and address problems, makes systems simpler to understand and manage, reduces the amount of time it takes to set up a product for production and provides for efficient flow of material through the manufacturing process. Costs incurred from overproduction, increased time spent in the manufacturing process, defective products, unnecessary transportation costs, and a higher than needed level of inventory are not intrinsic to a just-in-time system. These environments are generally able to stay more competitive within the marketplace.

36. D: Capacity constraint resource. The drum-buffer-rope (DBR) system is a methodology for scheduling operations based on the Theory of Constraints. In the production process, DBR assumes that the least capable physical resource, called the capacity constraint resource (CCR), in the process is the determining factor in setting the entire production schedule. The CCR, therefore, sets the rhythm of production and is dubbed the "drum." Drums are likely to cause bottlenecks in the process, so the DBR's "rope" is the communication mechanism, such as a material release schedule, that sets the flow into the production process at a rate that the CCR can handle. The "buffer" sits between the drum and the rope to ensure that materials are in place and ready to be processed when the CCR is available to do the work. The buffer could also be a shipping schedule that helps ensure the end product is on time and orders are not delayed. Throughput is the rate at which an organization produces income.

37. A: Obtaining materials at a low cost and high quality. Value chain analysis looks at a business' various value-enhancing activities (value chain) to identify opportunities and threats, improve the strategic planning system and provide access to low cost financing. It determines how and when value is added to a company's goods or services, and how to gain competitive advantages. Businesses use value chain analysis to help them:

- Hire and retain quality employees by providing a reward
- Improve the research and development process by supporting innovation and cooperation
- Obtain materials on a timely basis, at the least cost and highest quality
- Enhance marketing and sales by identifying market segments, using innovative advertising techniques, finding additional distribution channels, and motivating the sales staff
- Provide quality customer service by listening to customer feedback, implementing guarantee and replacement policies, and providing customer education and training

Business process reengineering examines how an organization operates in an attempt to improve efficiency. Benchmarking allows an organization to look at what it does, how it does it, and compare it performance to other organizations.

38. B: Setting a budget and schedule for the program. Total quality management (TQM) encompasses quality, teamwork, proactive management philosophies, and process improvement. When these principles are applied effectively, TQM espouses there to be a constant and continual increase in the quality of products and services supplied. TQM programs are implemented in five stages – preparation, planning, assessment, implementation, and diversification. Check sheets are used to collect quantitative and qualitative data. A control chart is a statistical tool used to determine variations in processes and to help in the forecasting and management functions of an organization. Ishikawa diagrams show the causes of an event and displays relationships between variables and the related causes.

39. D: Kaizen. Kaizen improves an organization's processes by eliminating waste, timing production with customer needs, and standardizing job processes. Kaizen brings efficiency to the workforce by reducing manual labor and teaching employees to accomplish more by eliminating wasted movement and methods. Kaizen is the Japanese term for "continuous improvement." Attention to efficiency and productivity of the workforce is key to Kaizen. Best practice analysis is the continuous search to improve an organization's processes and procedures by looking at other organizations that are considered to be the best in the industry. Generic benchmarking analyzes activities that are used by most organizations and compares performance in order to reengineer business processes. The Pareto principle states that 80% of the consequences derive from 20% of the causes.

40. C: Increase of customer base. Benchmarking is a method an organization uses to improve its operations by looking at what it does and how it functions, and comparing its performance to other organizations. First, an organization needs to determine which processes or activities to benchmark. Then, it selects the other organizations against which it wants to benchmark itself Information is collected, analyzed, and improvements to processes are determined. Finally, plans are put into place to re-engineer processes and the results of the changes are monitored.

41. C: Organizational structure. Internal control consists of:

- A control environment— structure for employee integrity, organizational competence, management operating style, and oversight by the board of directors
- Risk assessment— identification, analysis, and management of uncertainty meeting the organization's financial, compliance, and operational objectives
- Control activities— policies and procedures to address risk areas and provide safeguards against harmful actions
- Information— identification, collection, and exchange of financial, operational, and compliance information in a timely manner
- Monitoring— assessment of the quality of internal controls and providing. information about problem areas a control system

42. A: Foreign Corrupt Practices Act of 1977. The Foreign Corrupt Practices Act prevents illegal acts by U.S. organizations that deal with foreign nations. The Act prohibits the use of bribery as a means of obtaining or keeping business relationships. It also requires that organizations under the jurisdiction of the Securities and Exchange Commission maintain adequate systems of internal control. The main emphasis is on keeping records and accounts of all transactions to ensure that corrupt payments cannot be hidden in financial records. The Sarbanes-Oxley Act protects shareholders from corporation's fraudulent accounting activities. It strengthened the regulation of auditors, increased corporate responsibility for fraudulent actions, and provided for more disclosure of corporate financial statements.

43. A: Determining compliance with laws and regulations. A company undertakes an internal audit to verify accuracy and thoroughness of its financial records. This audit is performed by an internal member of the company, such as a Chief Financial Officer or controller. Internal audits determine if the company's policies and procedures are being followed, and if any illegal activity, such as embezzlement, has occurred. An internal audit discloses how well, or poorly, goals are being met, and whether the company is in compliance with laws and regulations. An internal audit may determine if; sound procurement practices are followed, resources have been properly maintained and utilized, operating procedures are efficient and followed, adequate management control systems exist, and areas of redundancy.

44. C: Gap analysis. Gap analysis compares actual performance against potential performance by examining the resources a company uses and the company's potential. The goal is to improve how efficiently resources are used and determine optimum resource usage. Quality audits are an examination of a quality system, executed on a regular basis to ensure compliance with a company's internal quality monitoring procedures. Corrective action is taken when standards are not met. An operational audit evaluates how well the management of an organization has conformed to organizational policies and budgets. A compliance audit determines if a company is following its own written policies as well as the laws, regulations, policies and procedures set by regulators.

45. D: Use external auditors to determine proper monitoring procedures. Developing and maintaining a control system for an information system requires:

- Identification of activities that pose a risk to the thoroughness and accuracy of financial reports
- Employee training in the proper use of information technology
- Written policies for the minimization of errors and misunderstandings

Once the system is in place, it needs to be monitored and audited to properly handle high risk areas.

46. B: Correct performance of applications. Processing controls help ensure that applications perform as expected by verifying that data is processed by authorized users, all data is accounted for, and no unauthorized data is added into the system. Input controls secure data and involve tools to make sure that data added to the system is from an authorized user, is properly formatted, and that it hasn't been lost or improperly changed. Output controls help ensure that data is displayed correctly; from data appearing on a computer monitor to printed data, reports, downloaded files and other information that is processed in some manner. Storage controls help ensure that data is backed up on a regular basis.

47. C: Assignment of recovery tasks to key employees. The goal of a disaster recovery plan is to keep important data secure in the event of a catastrophe. People implement the plan, therefore a method of contacting the key employees and assigning tasks to begin the recovery process is vital to a successful plan. The plan must consider every contingency, including pro-active, preventive measures such as routine backups of data, offsite storage of backed up data, and moving computer operations to a new location. Every action that is needed to recreate the data, software, and hardware is detailed in the plan, and an alternate site should be detailed should operations need to relocate due to disaster.

48. D: Setting standards of competence, confidentiality, integrity, and credibility. The Institute of Management Accountants (IMA) Statement of Ethical Professional Practice outlines four standards of conduct for its members— competence, confidentiality, integrity and credibility. The IMA states that a member's failure to comply with those standards may result in disciplinary action. The IMA also espouses four ethical principles— honesty, fairness, objectivity and responsibility. IMA members are expected to act in accordance with those principles and encourage others in their organizations to likewise adhere to them. In addition, the IMA's Statement of Ethical Professional Practice contains steps to resolve ethical conflict which are suggested should the established policies of the workplace prove unsuccessful.

49. B: Continuing education, compliance with laws, decision support information and good judgment. The Institute of Management Accountants (IMA) outlines four areas in which a management accountant must demonstrate competence. Management accountant who are IMA members have the following responsibilities with respect to competence:

- Keeping professional expertise and knowledge base current and up-to-date through continual education and skill development
- Performing jobs in compliance with laws, regulations and standards
- Contribute accurate and timely information to aid in decision making
- Recognizing potential conflicts of interest or constraints that may impact judgment or completion of a project and effectively communicating them to decision makers

50. A: Providing fair and objective information. The Institute of Management Accountants (IMA) outlines three areas in which a management accountant must act with credibility. Management accountant who are IMA members have the following responsibilities with respect to credibility:

- Communication of information objectively and without bias to clients and the public
- Disclosure of all relevant information which influences decision making and understanding of reports, analyses or recommendations
- Disclosure of deficiencies, delays or activities not conforming to organizational policy or applicable laws

Essay Question Responses

Answer 1

a. DM expenses = $205,000 for 10,000 kg

DM price variance = (actual DM expense) – (actual qty x standard price)

= ($205,000) – (10,000 kg x $19/kg) = $15,000 unfavorable

DM actual qty used = 400 kg + 10,000 kg – 250 kg = 10,150 kg

DM standard qty used = 49,000 knives x (200 g / knife) = 9,800 kg

DM quantity variance = (actual qty used x standard price) – (standard qty used x standard price)

= (10,150 kg x $19/kg) – (9,800 kg x $19/kg) = $6,650 unfavorable

DM total variance = DM price variance + DM quantity variance = $21,650 unfavorable

b. The unfavorable DM price variance could be due to a change in the market price of steel as a commodity, a certain contractual condition which Zurich Corp. has with its steel suppliers, an inability to find superior bidders for steel suppliers, poor planning in purchasing large quantities of steel so as to obtain a large-quantity discount, or other factors.

The unfavorable DM quantity variance could be due to a poor estimation of the steel required to produce a new knife, excess waste resulting from inefficiency in the manufacturing machinery or in the laborers, defects in finished products requiring their disposal, or other factors.
c. The Zurich Corp. leadership can probe these questions further to determine the most likely culprits for the variances. If the causes are outside of the company's control, then the standard figures should be adjusted to match reality. But insofar as the causes are within its control—such as concerning a poor supplier contract, inefficiency in the machinery or laborers, or defective finished products—the leadership should take action and enact policies to improve these factors of production.

Answer 2

a. Total DL hours = 300 laborers x 165 hrs/laborer = 49,500 hrs

DL rate variance = (actual hrs x actual wages) – (actual hrs x standard wages)

= (49,500 hrs x $11/hr) – (49,500 hrs x $12/hr) = $49,500 favorable

Standard DL hours = 1 hr/knife x 49,000 knives = 49,000 hrs

DL efficiency variance = (actual hrs x standard wages) – (standard hrs x standard wages)

= (49,500 hrs x $12/hr) – (49,000 hrs x $12/hr) = $6,000 unfavorable

DL total variance = DL rate variance + DL efficiency variance = $43,500 favorable

b. The favorable DL rate variance may be due to greater turnover in the labor force of more experienced or otherwise more highly compensated employees, a lesser need for overtime or weekend hours, more ownership-favorable negotiations with collective labor, or other factors.

The unfavorable DL efficiency variance may be due to ongoing inefficiency in the machinery requiring slightly more labor hours for each knife, specific cases of inefficiency (e.g. an accident) requiring the temporary ceasing of production, a lack of proper training in the labor force, a lack of proper supervision or management, or other factors.

c. Because the DL total variance is favorable the Zurich Corp. leadership might be inclined to ignore improving the process—or, more likely, the leadership might be inclined to ignore possible improvements in the DL rate variance. But it would be wise for them, while focusing on drilling down to improve the efficiency variance, to nevertheless also seek improvements in the rate variance as is feasible. The efficiency variance could be improved by assessing the efficiency of the production process (e.g., in terms of machine downtime and worker breaks), while the leadership could also analyze what caused the favorable rate variance so as to ensure continued favorable variances in that amount. On the other hand, a favorable rate variance could be due to an incorrect standard wage for labor, in which case the standard figures need to be updated moving forward.

Answer 3

a. VOH expenses = $255,000 for 49,500 DL hrs

VOH spending variance = (actual VOH expenses) – (actual DL hrs x standard VOH cost)

= ($255,000) – (49,500 hrs x $5.00/hr) = $7,500 unfavorable

Standard VOH hrs = 1.1 hrs/knife x 49,000 knives = 53,900 hrs

VOH efficiency variance = (actual DL hrs x standard VOH cost) – (standard VOH hrs x standard VOH cost)

= (49,5000 hrs x $5.00/hr) – (53,900 hrs x $5.00/hr) = $22,000 favorable

VOH total variance = VOH spending variance + VOH efficiency variance = $14,500 favorable

b. The VOH spending variance can be due to a misclassification of certain cost accounts (which should not have been included in VOH), changes in utility prices, mistakes in the depreciation accounting for fixed assets, or other factors.

The VOH efficiency variance can be due to machinery efficiency exceeding expectations, higher-quality direct materials, an underestimation of labor efficiency (e.g. surpassing learning curve expectations), or other factors.

c. The Zurich Corp. leadership should first address its variance issues according to the dollar extent of the variances, devoting more initial attention as the variance is more unfavorable. But the leadership's attention and energy should not necessarily be ultimately devoted proportionately to the degree of the variance, as it also depends on how improvable the variances are and how time-intensive the implementation of these improvements will be. Depending on the circumstances and available solutions, the leadership could possibly improve the DL rate variance substantially while making hardly a dent in the DM price variance. It is up to the leadership's discretion on how best to address these issues, after best investigating the causes of the variances.

Answer 4

The Zurich Corporation could also conduct analyses of fixed overhead variances, whether spending or volume, to learn of favorable or unfavorable cost conditions pertaining to taxes (particularly property taxes), rent, and insurance. Additionally, the business could look into sales variances, divided into price and volume variance—and the latter divided further into sales mix and sales quantity variance. These sales variances would generate greater data to the business concerning its revenue and pricing. These are just two examples of further variances the Zurich Corporation could analyze.

Answer 5

Total sales = (12 x $90,000) + (8 x $110,000) = $1,960,000

Variable production cost per unit

Plus: ($30,000 + $13,000 + $6,000) = $49,000

Deluxe: ($42,000 + $15,000 + $6,000) = $63,000

Fixed production cost per unit

$120,000 / 30 units = $4,000

Variable-costing income:

Sales – COGS – fixed overhead - GS&A = net income

= $1,960,000 – ($49,000 x 12 + $63,000 x 8) - $120,000 - $250,000 = $498,000

Absorption-costing income:

Sales – COGS (incl. fixed cost) – GS&A = net income

= $1,960,000 – (($49,000 + $4,000) x 12 + ($63,000 + $4,000) x 8) - $250,000 = $538,000

Answer 6

While absorption costing can be helpful in its assigning of all production costs to products, its blurring of the distinction between fixed and variable costs can cause difficulties for the Smith Equipment Co. decision-makers. Since fixed overhead costs by definition are the same for varying levels of production, it would be unhelpful for the company leadership to allocate fixed overhead on a per-unit basis when making decisions related to cost, volume, and profit. Furthermore, as Smith's statement shows, the usage of absorption costing creates an artificial increase in income because of the portion of fixed overhead which is allocated to inventory rather than incurred as a period expense. This is especially relevant to avoid any perverse incentives for managers to ramp up production without the change affecting the current-period income statements. Lastly, variable costing would help the Smith Equipment Co. leadership to better compare the Plus and Deluxe product lines, since there would not be a fixed overhead cost distorting the true per-unit cost for each line.

On the other hand, there is logic behind the assigning of all production costs to one's products, especially in a case like Smith's where production was intentionally increased in anticipation of the subsequent quarter's sales. For this reason, it would be more fitting to use absorption costing so as to assign a portion of the recent quarter's total production costs to the bulldozers actually manufactured in that quarter. And this all is independent of the fact that absorption costing, not variable, is GAAP-compliant.

Answer 7

Unless Smith Equipment Co. produces distinctly customized bulldozers with differing functions and characteristics for different customers as an ordinary matter of course, the homogeneity of their products—all their bulldozers being grouped into one of two product lines—makes process costing to be much more appropriate for accurately tracking their production expenses. Job-order costing is more appropriate for a manufacturing process where each product is heterogeneous in some manner, and hence where it would be unhelpful to group differing manufacturing processes into one cost pool for decision-making purposes.

Answer 8

The leadership needs pro forma financial statements, that is, financial statements for the potential lender projecting how Smith Equipment Co. will profit from a loan, and especially a pro forma income statement. Depending on the requirements of the bank, other pro forma financial statements should be prepared, such as a balance sheet and statement of cash flows. The preparation of this information will require analyzing previous and current financial data for the business. For example, accounts receivable can be projected according to the estimated change in sales and the company's average collection time for outstanding accounts, and sales can be projected according to estimated profitability of business ventures made possible by the new loan capital.

How to Overcome Test Anxiety

Just the thought of taking a test is enough to make most people a little nervous. A test is an important event that can have a long-term impact on your future, so it's important to take it seriously and it's natural to feel anxious about performing well. But just because anxiety is normal, that doesn't mean that it's helpful in test taking, or that you should simply accept it as part of your life. Anxiety can have a variety of effects. These effects can be mild, like making you feel slightly nervous, or severe, like blocking your ability to focus or remember even a simple detail.

If you experience test anxiety—whether severe or mild—it's important to know how to beat it. To discover this, first you need to understand what causes test anxiety.

Causes of Test Anxiety

While we often think of anxiety as an uncontrollable emotional state, it can actually be caused by simple, practical things. One of the most common causes of test anxiety is that a person does not feel adequately prepared for their test. This feeling can be the result of many different issues such as poor study habits or lack of organization, but the most common culprit is time management. Starting to study too late, failing to organize your study time to cover all of the material, or being distracted while you study will mean that you're not well prepared for the test. This may lead to cramming the night before, which will cause you to be physically and mentally exhausted for the test. Poor time management also contributes to feelings of stress, fear, and hopelessness as you realize you are not well prepared but don't know what to do about it.

Other times, test anxiety is not related to your preparation for the test but comes from unresolved fear. This may be a past failure on a test, or poor performance on tests in general. It may come from comparing yourself to others who seem to be performing better or from the stress of living up to expectations. Anxiety may be driven by fears of the future—how failure on this test would affect your educational and career goals. These fears are often completely irrational, but they can still negatively impact your test performance.

Review Video: 3 Reasons You Have Test Anxiety
Visit mometrix.com/academy and enter code: 428468

Elements of Test Anxiety

As mentioned earlier, test anxiety is considered to be an emotional state, but it has physical and mental components as well. Sometimes you may not even realize that you are suffering from test anxiety until you notice the physical symptoms. These can include trembling hands, rapid heartbeat, sweating, nausea, and tense muscles. Extreme anxiety may lead to fainting or vomiting. Obviously, any of these symptoms can have a negative impact on testing. It is important to recognize them as soon as they begin to occur so that you can address the problem before it damages your performance.

Review Video: 3 Ways to Tell You Have Test Anxiety
Visit mometrix.com/academy and enter code: 927847

The mental components of test anxiety include trouble focusing and inability to remember learned information. During a test, your mind is on high alert, which can help you recall information and stay focused for an extended period of time. However, anxiety interferes with your mind's natural processes, causing you to blank out, even on the questions you know well. The strain of testing during anxiety makes it difficult to stay focused, especially on a test that may take several hours. Extreme anxiety can take a huge mental toll, making it difficult not only to recall test information but even to understand the test questions or pull your thoughts together.

Review Video: How Test Anxiety Affects Memory
Visit mometrix.com/academy and enter code: 609003

Effects of Test Anxiety

Test anxiety is like a disease—if left untreated, it will get progressively worse. Anxiety leads to poor performance, and this reinforces the feelings of fear and failure, which in turn lead to poor performances on subsequent tests. It can grow from a mild nervousness to a crippling condition. If allowed to progress, test anxiety can have a big impact on your schooling, and consequently on your future.

Test anxiety can spread to other parts of your life. Anxiety on tests can become anxiety in any stressful situation, and blanking on a test can turn into panicking in a job situation. But fortunately, you don't have to let anxiety rule your testing and determine your grades. There are a number of relatively simple steps you can take to move past anxiety and function normally on a test and in the rest of life.

Review Video: How Test Anxiety Impacts Your Grades
Visit mometrix.com/academy and enter code: 939819

Physical Steps for Beating Test Anxiety

While test anxiety is a serious problem, the good news is that it can be overcome. It doesn't have to control your ability to think and remember information. While it may take time, you can begin taking steps today to beat anxiety.

Just as your first hint that you may be struggling with anxiety comes from the physical symptoms, the first step to treating it is also physical. Rest is crucial for having a clear, strong mind. If you are tired, it is much easier to give in to anxiety. But if you establish good sleep habits, your body and mind will be ready to perform optimally, without the strain of exhaustion. Additionally, sleeping well helps you to retain information better, so you're more likely to recall the answers when you see the test questions.

Getting good sleep means more than going to bed on time. It's important to allow your brain time to relax. Take study breaks from time to time so it doesn't get overworked, and don't study right before bed. Take time to rest your mind before trying to rest your body, or you may find it difficult to fall asleep.

Review Video: The Importance of Sleep for Your Brain
Visit mometrix.com/academy and enter code: 319338

Along with sleep, other aspects of physical health are important in preparing for a test. Good nutrition is vital for good brain function. Sugary foods and drinks may give a burst of energy but this burst is followed by a crash, both physically and emotionally. Instead, fuel your body with protein and vitamin-rich foods.

Also, drink plenty of water. Dehydration can lead to headaches and exhaustion, especially if your brain is already under stress from the rigors of the test. Particularly if your test is a long one, drink water during the breaks. And if possible, take an energy-boosting snack to eat between sections.

Review Video: How Diet Can Affect your Mood
Visit mometrix.com/academy and enter code: 624317

Along with sleep and diet, a third important part of physical health is exercise. Maintaining a steady workout schedule is helpful, but even taking 5-minute study breaks to walk can help get your blood pumping faster and clear your head. Exercise also releases endorphins, which contribute to a positive feeling and can help combat test anxiety.

When you nurture your physical health, you are also contributing to your mental health. If your body is healthy, your mind is much more likely to be healthy as well. So take time to rest, nourish your body with healthy food and water, and get moving as much as possible. Taking these physical steps will make you stronger and more able to take the mental steps necessary to overcome test anxiety.

Mental Steps for Beating Test Anxiety

Working on the mental side of test anxiety can be more challenging, but as with the physical side, there are clear steps you can take to overcome it. As mentioned earlier, test anxiety often stems from lack of preparation, so the obvious solution is to prepare for the test. Effective studying may be the most important weapon you have for beating test anxiety, but you can and should employ several other mental tools to combat fear.

First, boost your confidence by reminding yourself of past success—tests or projects that you aced. If you're putting as much effort into preparing for this test as you did for those, there's no reason you should expect to fail here. Work hard to prepare; then trust your preparation.

Second, surround yourself with encouraging people. It can be helpful to find a study group, but be sure that the people you're around will encourage a positive attitude. If you spend time with others who are anxious or cynical, this will only contribute to your own anxiety. Look for others who are motivated to study hard from a desire to succeed, not from a fear of failure.

Third, reward yourself. A test is physically and mentally tiring, even without anxiety, and it can be helpful to have something to look forward to. Plan an activity following the test, regardless of the outcome, such as going to a movie or getting ice cream.

When you are taking the test, if you find yourself beginning to feel anxious, remind yourself that you know the material. Visualize successfully completing the test. Then take a few deep, relaxing breaths and return to it. Work through the questions carefully but with confidence, knowing that you are capable of succeeding.

Developing a healthy mental approach to test taking will also aid in other areas of life. Test anxiety affects more than just the actual test—it can be damaging to your mental health and even contribute to depression. It's important to beat test anxiety before it becomes a problem for more than testing.

Review Video: Test Anxiety and Depression
Visit mometrix.com/academy and enter code: 904704

Study Strategy

Being prepared for the test is necessary to combat anxiety, but what does being prepared look like? You may study for hours on end and still not feel prepared. What you need is a strategy for test prep. The next few pages outline our recommended steps to help you plan out and conquer the challenge of preparation.

Step 1: Scope Out the Test

Learn everything you can about the format (multiple choice, essay, etc.) and what will be on the test. Gather any study materials, course outlines, or sample exams that may be available. Not only will this help you to prepare, but knowing what to expect can help to alleviate test anxiety.

Step 2: Map Out the Material

Look through the textbook or study guide and make note of how many chapters or sections it has. Then divide these over the time you have. For example, if a book has 15 chapters and you have five days to study, you need to cover three chapters each day. Even better, if you have the time, leave an extra day at the end for overall review after you have gone through the material in depth.

If time is limited, you may need to prioritize the material. Look through it and make note of which sections you think you already have a good grasp on, and which need review. While you are studying, skim quickly through the familiar sections and take more time on the challenging parts. Write out your plan so you don't get lost as you go. Having a written plan also helps you feel more in control of the study, so anxiety is less likely to arise from feeling overwhelmed at the amount to cover.

Step 3: Gather Your Tools

Decide what study method works best for you. Do you prefer to highlight in the book as you study and then go back over the highlighted portions? Or do you type out notes of the important information? Or is it helpful to make flashcards that you can carry with you? Assemble the pens, index cards, highlighters, post-it notes, and any other materials you may need so you won't be distracted by getting up to find things while you study.

If you're having a hard time retaining the information or organizing your notes, experiment with different methods. For example, try color-coding by subject with colored pens, highlighters, or post-it notes. If you learn better by hearing, try recording yourself reading your notes so you can listen while in the car, working out, or simply sitting at your desk. Ask a friend to quiz you from your flashcards, or try teaching someone the material to solidify it in your mind.

Step 4: Create Your Environment

It's important to avoid distractions while you study. This includes both the obvious distractions like visitors and the subtle distractions like an uncomfortable chair (or a too-comfortable couch that makes you want to fall asleep). Set up the best study environment possible: good lighting and a comfortable work area. If background music helps you focus, you may want to turn it on, but otherwise keep the room quiet. If you are using a computer to take notes, be sure you don't have any other windows open, especially applications like social media, games, or anything else that could distract you. Silence your phone and turn off notifications. Be sure to keep water close by so you stay hydrated while you study (but avoid unhealthy drinks and snacks).

Also, take into account the best time of day to study. Are you freshest first thing in the morning? Try to set aside some time then to work through the material. Is your mind clearer in the afternoon or evening? Schedule your study session then. Another method is to study at the same time of day that you will take the test, so that your brain gets used to working on the material at that time and will be ready to focus at test time.

Step 5: Study!

Once you have done all the study preparation, it's time to settle into the actual studying. Sit down, take a few moments to settle your mind so you can focus, and begin to follow your study plan. Don't give in to distractions or let yourself procrastinate. This is your time to prepare so you'll be ready to fearlessly approach the test. Make the most of the time and stay focused.

Of course, you don't want to burn out. If you study too long you may find that you're not retaining the information very well. Take regular study breaks. For example, taking five minutes out of every hour to walk briskly, breathing deeply and swinging your arms, can help your mind stay fresh.

As you get to the end of each chapter or section, it's a good idea to do a quick review. Remind yourself of what you learned and work on any difficult parts. When you feel that you've mastered the material, move on to the next part. At the end of your study session, briefly skim through your notes again.

But while review is helpful, cramming last minute is NOT. If at all possible, work ahead so that you won't need to fit all your study into the last day. Cramming overloads your brain with more information than it can process and retain, and your tired mind may struggle to recall even previously learned information when it is overwhelmed with last-minute study. Also, the urgent nature of cramming and the stress placed on your brain contribute to anxiety. You'll be more likely to go to the test feeling unprepared and having trouble thinking clearly.

So don't cram, and don't stay up late before the test, even just to review your notes at a leisurely pace. Your brain needs rest more than it needs to go over the information again. In fact, plan to finish your studies by noon or early afternoon the day before the test. Give your brain the rest of the day to relax or focus on other things, and get a good night's sleep. Then you will be fresh for the test and better able to recall what you've studied.

Step 6: Take a practice test

Many courses offer sample tests, either online or in the study materials. This is an excellent resource to check whether you have mastered the material, as well as to prepare for the test format and environment.

Check the test format ahead of time: the number of questions, the type (multiple choice, free response, etc.), and the time limit. Then create a plan for working through them. For example, if you have 30 minutes to take a 60-question test, your limit is 30 seconds per question. Spend less time on the questions you know well so that you can take more time on the difficult ones.

If you have time to take several practice tests, take the first one open book, with no time limit. Work through the questions at your own pace and make sure you fully understand them. Gradually work up to taking a test under test conditions: sit at a desk with all study materials put away and set a timer. Pace yourself to make sure you finish the test with time to spare and go back to check your answers if you have time.

After each test, check your answers. On the questions you missed, be sure you understand why you missed them. Did you misread the question (tests can use tricky wording)? Did you forget the information? Or was it something you hadn't learned? Go back and study any shaky areas that the practice tests reveal.

Taking these tests not only helps with your grade, but also aids in combating test anxiety. If you're already used to the test conditions, you're less likely to worry about it, and working through tests until you're scoring well gives you a confidence boost. Go through the practice tests until you feel comfortable, and then you can go into the test knowing that you're ready for it.

Test Tips

On test day, you should be confident, knowing that you've prepared well and are ready to answer the questions. But aside from preparation, there are several test day strategies you can employ to maximize your performance.

First, as stated before, get a good night's sleep the night before the test (and for several nights before that, if possible). Go into the test with a fresh, alert mind rather than staying up late to study.

Try not to change too much about your normal routine on the day of the test. It's important to eat a nutritious breakfast, but if you normally don't eat breakfast at all, consider eating just a protein bar. If you're a coffee drinker, go ahead and have your normal coffee. Just make sure you time it so that the caffeine doesn't wear off right in the middle of your test. Avoid sugary beverages, and drink enough water to stay hydrated but not so much that you need a restroom break 10 minutes into the test. If your test isn't first thing in the morning, consider going for a walk or doing a light workout before the test to get your blood flowing.

Allow yourself enough time to get ready, and leave for the test with plenty of time to spare so you won't have the anxiety of scrambling to arrive in time. Another reason to be early is to select a good seat. It's helpful to sit away from doors and windows, which can be distracting. Find a good seat, get out your supplies, and settle your mind before the test begins.

When the test begins, start by going over the instructions carefully, even if you already know what to expect. Make sure you avoid any careless mistakes by following the directions.

Then begin working through the questions, pacing yourself as you've practiced. If you're not sure on an answer, don't spend too much time on it, and don't let it shake your confidence. Either skip it and come back later, or eliminate as many wrong answers as possible and guess among the remaining ones. Don't dwell on these questions as you continue—put them out of your mind and focus on what lies ahead.

Be sure to read all of the answer choices, even if you're sure the first one is the right answer. Sometimes you'll find a better one if you keep reading. But don't second-guess yourself if you do immediately know the answer. Your gut instinct is usually right. Don't let test anxiety rob you of the information you know.

If you have time at the end of the test (and if the test format allows), go back and review your answers. Be cautious about changing any, since your first instinct tends to be correct, but make sure you didn't misread any of the questions or accidentally mark the wrong answer choice. Look over any you skipped and make an educated guess.

At the end, leave the test feeling confident. You've done your best, so don't waste time worrying about your performance or wishing you could change anything. Instead, celebrate the successful completion of this test. And finally, use this test to learn how to deal with anxiety even better next time.

Review Video: 5 Tips to Beat Test Anxiety
Visit mometrix.com/academy and enter code: 570656

Important Qualification

Not all anxiety is created equal. If your test anxiety is causing major issues in your life beyond the classroom or testing center, or if you are experiencing troubling physical symptoms related to your anxiety, it may be a sign of a serious physiological or psychological condition. If this sounds like your situation, we strongly encourage you to seek professional help.

Thank You

We at Mometrix would like to extend our heartfelt thanks to you, our friend and patron, for allowing us to play a part in your journey. It is a privilege to serve people from all walks of life who are unified in their commitment to building the best future they can for themselves.

The preparation you devote to these important testing milestones may be the most valuable educational opportunity you have for making a real difference in your life. We encourage you to put your heart into it—that feeling of succeeding, overcoming, and yes, conquering will be well worth the hours you've invested.

We want to hear your story, your struggles and your successes, and if you see any opportunities for us to improve our materials so we can help others even more effectively in the future, please share that with us as well. **The team at Mometrix would be absolutely thrilled to hear from you!** So please, send us an email (support@mometrix.com) and let's stay in touch.

If you'd like some additional help, check out these other resources we offer for your exam:
http://MometrixFlashcards.com/CMA

Additional Bonus Material

Due to our efforts to try to keep this book to a manageable length, we've created a link that will give you access to all of your additional bonus material:

mometrix.com/bonus948/cmap1fppc